Get Your Head Out of Your App

Get Your Head Out of Your App

A Psychic's Guide to Keeping and Attracting True Love

Deborah Graham

Health Communications, Inc.
Deerfield Beach, Florida

www.hcibooks.com

Library of Congress Cataloging-in-Publication Data
is available through the Library of Congress

© 2015 Deborah Graham

ISBN-13: 978-07573-1874-0 (Paperback)
ISBN-10: 07573-1874-6 (Paperback)
ISBN-13: 978-07573-1875-7 (ePub)
ISBN-10: 07573-1875-4 (ePub)

HCI, its logos, and marks are trademarks of Health Communications, Inc.

Publisher: Health Communications, Inc.
      3201 S.W. 15th Street
      Deerfield Beach, FL 33442–8190

Cover design by Larissa Hise Henoch
Interior design and formatting by Lawna Patterson Oldfield

Contents

Introduction 1

Chapter 1 Disconnected: The New Normal 7

Chapter 2 Creating Healthier Relationship
Patterns: The Story of Camilla
and Michael 25

Chapter 3 Setting a Goal: Finding a
Soul Mate 49

Chapter 4 The Twin Flame: The Story of
Danielle and Andrew 73

Chapter 5 The Rule of Three 93

Chapter 6 The First Date: Tapping into
the Other Person's Energy 105

Chapter 7   How to Keep the
Energy Flowing 121

Chapter 8   The Signs of an Energy
Vampire 149

Chapter 9   When to Say Good-bye
to Someone and Hello to
Yourself Again 167

A Closing Thought 185

Introduction

I don't believe in coincidences; I believe in destiny and that everyone—absolutely and without a doubt—has a soul mate. But being ready to find that soul mate and being ready to accept love from that soul mate isn't a walk in the park. Cinderella was a big fat liar: Prince Charming isn't going to fall from the sky onto your lap ready to whisk you away on his pristine steed, and Cinderella isn't waiting around in a tiny cottage for you to stumble upon her one day and swoop her up. You can't expect it all to just happen *for* you. But this doesn't mean that fairy tales can't become real. I'm here to tell you they can. They *are* real, and you can make your life a fairy tale just by being your best you.

For the last twenty years I have been working as a psychic matchmaker. I have matched thousands of individuals with their soul mates and helped them to sustain lasting relationships. I'm not a dating service—if you're looking to learn how to date, you've come to the wrong book. My life's work is about helping you find the one particular person with whom you feel the highest high of your life—the true twin flame of your soul, the individual with whom you can't even see another person in the room and whose absence makes you want to throw up because you feel such an extreme physical ache: the strongest connection of your life.

When I tell people that I'm a psychic matchmaker, they don't always understand what that means. I don't look into a magical crystal ball to predict the future; I read people's energy, their auras, the forces that radiate from them. This is something we all can do, but I have been given a gift from God that allows me to be more sensitive to the vibrations of others. I believe that I was given this gift so that I can help people find their purpose in life.

When I make a match, I don't connect from the outside, from what people tell me about themselves, or from what they tell me they want; I do it from the inside. I see beautiful love from within people—love and power and the essence of who they are—and I connect with that and feel their lives. By tapping into the solar plexus chakra (where an individual's essence is contained), I am able to pair a person with a match that will last a lifetime. But in order for you to achieve that, you must first do a lot of clearing away—clear away the past, doubts, fears, and preconceived notions about the exterior appearance of your mate.

In my life, I have matched thousands of individuals from all walks of life with each other. It hasn't just been individuals who are in the earlier stages of life and are fresh to the dating scene; I have matched people who were married before, sometimes for thirty years, who lost their marriage partners through either death or divorce. I've matched not only men with women but also men with men and women with women. And I've helped people who are in all different stages of relationship with themselves. It doesn't matter if you're tall, short, male, female, plus size, or size zero—love is out there. It's just about making yourself ready for love. My work is to help you do that.

It doesn't matter what your past is like; you have to figure out your own desires and find strength and power within. You have to allow that to happen because it is part of your journey. But in order to do that you have to pull the weeds away from your heart and soul, and keep pulling. It doesn't matter how good you look—you have got to feel love from within. If you can create positive, vibrant energy within yourself, you will emit positive vibrations; your magnetic field will strengthen and grow. But if you believe that life sucks, it *will* suck, and you'll never find what you're looking for.

> If you can create vibrant energy within yourself, you will emit positive vibrations.

I have had a client for almost a year named Jill. She's a very attractive woman, but she didn't know it. She had no confidence in herself. As a result, she kept going out with the wrong guys because she thought she needed to be with someone who needed her. I discovered that Jill was even going so far as to change her hair color to the color preferred by the person she was dating! Instead of leading with her intuition, she was leading with her insecurity. It took a lot of work, a lot of time, and a lot of coaching before Jill was able to get sexy *for herself.*

She started by reminding herself of the following every night for four months: "I am beautiful. I am love. I am light. I am whole." She started to be able to love herself from the inside. Jill came out of her cocoon and blossomed into an incredible butterfly because of the work that she did. She was able to open herself up and discover what had been driving her to do the things she did in order to keep a man in her life. She stopped trying to be with a person who would love her hair and her body and started to learn to be in love with herself.

By using the mantras, getting rid of the layers of pain she carried, doing some deep soul work, and forgiving everyone who ever hurt her, Jill became stronger and more confident. Her eyes became brighter and her physical body changed—and this time not because she changed them with beauty products. Her features changed because she grew to respect and love herself. Through this work, Jill was able to find a connection with a man who loves her just as she is, and they are now married.

Just like Jill, you will need patience to change your situation. Finding yourself and your soul mate is like making a baby. You don't just get pregnant and then immediately have a child. It takes nine months to make a baby inside your body. The reality is that anything worth working on is worth waiting on. It may take nine months; it may take nine years. You have to put the energy out there and be patient.

Twenty-two years ago, I had two particular clients. One was a man who had lost his wife of thirty years whom he loved deeply. He was about seventy-two at the time, and he came in because he wanted to see where his life was going, so we began working together. I could see that he wanted to find love again, someone who would be his true partner. The other client was a woman of sixty-eight who had lost her husband of about thirty years. She too was looking for love. So I scheduled their appointments at the same time on the same day.

I had another client coming in before that, so these two people got to meet each other in the waiting room. When I finished with my first client, I came out and told them they should go on a date together and really meet each other. They asked me to go with them and even said they'd pay. So we all went together to a restaurant called Captain D's. I remember it was on a Wednesday and we had to go before 6:00 PM so they could get the senior discount. We ate and talked. Two years later they got married, and they were together until the day he died. On his deathbed, he told me that I had given him the best years of his life. After thirty years of marriage, he had finally found his soul mate and was at peace. You have to be ready to be patient.

So let me cut right to the chase: This book is not for the faint of heart. You either want to do the work of finding that connection or you don't—and this is *real work*. If you're not willing to put the energy into yourself, walk away right now. But if you are, buckle your seat belt for the ride of your life, because this book is all about you. That's right—finding your soul mate *must* mean finding yourself first and your soul mate second.

You can't just say, "If only I could have this man or this woman, I'd be happy." You just have to love *you*. Our lives are like trees: there are many branches, and some may fall off while others may grow. Life moves all on its own; it'll twist you left and right, up and down, north and south, east and west. The one truth we get is to find the center from within. If you can do that, the rest will come. Just remember that we are all going through a temporary human experience, and we aren't here for a long time, we're here for a good time!

Chapter 1

Disconnected: The New Normal

We are all here to learn. In everything we do, we have the opportunity to learn something new about ourselves and about the world we live in. I believe that technology can aid our learning in great ways: in just a few keystrokes it can give us answers to things that puzzle us, it can tell us how to boil an egg, and it can help us to stay in touch with faraway family members, to name just a few things. The problem comes, I think, when people expect technology to answer their questions about love, loneliness, and themselves and when people use technology to avoid getting in touch with themselves.

Let me give you an example. When you lose someone close to you, you're going to feel a wide range of feelings, from sadness all the way to anger. That's normal. That's grief. That's *human*. Anytime you experience a major change in your life, you're going to experience a wide array of emotions. You have two options: avoid those emotions or feel them. Technology makes it very easy for us to choose to avoid emotions, especially now that we carry that technology around with us in our pockets and our purses. Feeling nervous? Grab your smartphone! Feeling sad? Hop on the computer! It's easier than ever before to lose yourself in the cloud, and I'm not talking about the fluffy ones in the sky.

Be honest with me. Does your day look something like this schedule?

- Wake up to the alarm that you set on your phone.

- Check your phone for text messages, e-mails, and other notifications.

- Make coffee, brush your teeth, and shower.

- Check your phone for text messages, e-mails, and other notifications.

- Get dressed and leave for work.

- Get settled into the office and check the e-mail on your work computer.

- Work from 9:00 AM to 5:00 PM.

- Meet your best friend for dinner, and while you eat you both leave your phones out on the dinner table.

- Check your phone for text messages, e-mails, and other notifications while having dinner.

- Get home and change out of your work clothes.

- Check your phone for text messages, e-mails, and other notifications.

- Open a bottle of wine and turn on the TV.

- Check your phone for text messages, e-mails, and other notifications.

- Go to bed.

Does this sound about right? When you really think about it, how much of your day do you spend staring at a screen, waiting for or crafting a response to a ten-minute conversation you've been having all day through text messages? How much of your conversation with your best friend at dinner is about how a text-message conversation with a love interest got confused because someone didn't respond or you texted something sarcastically and the other person didn't know that this was the tone you intended? How much of what you talk about with coworkers is a reference to something you saw on Facebook? When was the last time you sat quietly with yourself and a cup of tea with nothing on and your phone put away?

> When was the last time you sat quietly with yourself and a cup of tea and your phone put away?

The OCT

People have become what I like to call OCTs: obsessive-compulsive texters. We all know them: these people will text you for two hours, back and forth and back and forth, but absolutely won't take your call, even though you know they're right by the phone because they *just* texted you. Are you one of those people?

People communicate with someone by phone because they want that person to listen to them. You could go back and forth for months texting with someone and never know whether you're actually connecting, because you're not hearing each other's voices or feeling each other's energy.

When I am creating a match with clients, I tell them not to take pictures of themselves and send them to each other and not to text back and forth. I tell them to pick up the phone and decide to meet for dinner—nothing more and nothing less, because they'll meet for real at dinner. And that's really what you want.

When you're texting or e-mailing, you have the ability to edit yourself and slowly craft the person you think the other person wants to be with. But when you're on the phone or in person, you're not able to edit. You're able to feel the energy of the other person, whether he or she is happy, sad, or angry. You can hear so much through a person's voice. You can just feel what's going on with someone you're talking to. But during a text message you can't feel what the person is feeling. It's a text message—it's a *computer* that's talking to you!

And why wouldn't that be the case? There's an app for everything—for love, relationships, and sex. Anything you want to have or want to know, you can Google it. People are using the Internet for any and everything—even shopping at online stores. We have connected with the online world to such a deep degree that we've lost ourselves. It's almost as though we live, eat, sleep, and breathe through our apps. If you're trying to find a recipe, that's a great time to use the Internet. I can never remember how long to boil an egg, so I look it up on the computer. But if you're trying to find a recipe for love, you're not going to find it in your apps or online. There is no app to yourself except you—you are your own eternal app.

The Texting Triangle

Since the advent of the Internet, we've lost that lovin' feeling of face-to-face interaction. We've lost communication with one another. We've lost that niche of connecting. We've been tangled into the triangle of the text-messaging world. Before, a conversation used to go like this:

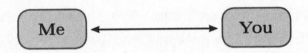

Now our conversations go like this:

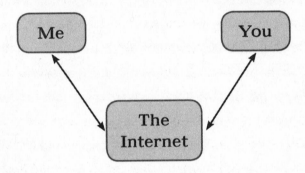

In the hectic shuffle of all the texting and all the computers, we've completely lost ourselves and one another. When it comes to a conversation, now we have a middleman: the Internet. Our devices are doing the work for us and coming between us and the people we're trying to talk to, to the extent that we're not even really talking to them anymore. We're tapping into the cloud with every conversation instead of tapping into the heart of another person.

And since we normally don't share our hearts with everyone, we protect ourselves because this middleman is present. While people still express their feelings and emotions, the energy behind those emotions is getting lost in the cloud. Rather than being able to use their own voices to put their feelings into words, people expect an image—a smiley face, a sad face, a thumbs-up—to express it *for* them. The difficult work of having to put your feelings into words is part of what helps you understand what your feelings are, and it helps the person to whom you're expressing them to feel more connected to you while listening and helping you understand what those feelings are.

Relationships have come to be like two ships passing in the night. People live their separate lives, but they're not really communicating together anymore. We send a text to say we love someone rather than expressing it verbally or nonverbally, rather than realizing that sometimes you don't even need to say anything—it's how you do it. Just going up to people and hugging them can say far more than any text message you could ever send. Having the bodily connection is incredibly important, as is knowing that you feel safe, which is something you can know only by being near the other person.

Texting has become an addiction for some people—just like alcohol and drugs—to the extent that they don't even realize the slippery slope they're on with their text-message conversations until they look up one day and realize that something is missing. But until that point, they're filled with the feeling that they constantly need to be texting.

> Texting has become an addiction for some people— just like alcohol and drugs.

Texting Relationships

Have you ever heard someone reluctantly say, "I think we have a texting relationship"? Do you find that people ask you to please look at them instead of at your phone? If so, this may be a good time to examine how you're communicating; you might be in danger of being an OCT.

In a texting relationship, there is minimal to no verbal communication. What that really means is that there's minimal to no *spiritual* communication. You're connecting with the data of the phone instead of the person. Ask yourself the following:

- Is there a person you text all the time? If not, congratulate yourself! You're not an OCT! If yes, ask yourself the next question.

- Do you talk to this person on the phone or face-to-face more than once a week? If yes, then great job! You're probably not an OCT! If not, ask yourself the next question.

- Do you expect this person to amuse and entertain you with the content of the text messages? If not, then it sounds like you're on the verge of becoming an OCT. In the future make sure that you try to refine your text messages to be about scheduling plans to see each other or talk on the phone, and include only tiny bits of actual information. If yes, then ask yourself the next question.

- Are you sure that the people you text are actually people and not just part of your phone? This sounds like a silly question—of course they're people! But take a minute and try to remember the last time you saw or talked to them. What do they look like? What do they sound like? Do they hunch their shoulders when they're feeling uncomfortable, or do they stretch their bodies out in a chair? If you don't know the answer or are struggling to recall it, you're probably in danger of both having a texting relationship with someone and being an OCT, because this is what's happening: you're creating a connection with the cloud rather than reaching into yourself and the other person and connecting with his or her spirit.

Technological Convenience

Most of us want everything right now, and we've come to live in a world where we can get just about everything right now. Is there a book you want to read? There's no longer any need to go to a bookstore to find it—if there even is a bookstore near you anymore. Now you can simply go online and download an entire book onto your computer or tablet. You can even have groceries delivered to your house. Everything from shampoo to dining room tables is available with a few clicks on a computer screen. It's truly amazing how convenient technology has made the world, and that's not all bad.

The problem comes when we expect our relationships to be convenient. That's not realistic. Relationships aren't a matter of convenience; they're hard work and energy. You're losing the personal connection if you have this expectation, and you're losing yourself. You're not actually giving someone your time if you're sending a text message. If you can make the time to think of someone and send a text message, you can pick up the darn phone and talk. If that person doesn't want to pick up the phone and talk to you, then nine times out of ten, that person really doesn't want to be with you.

> **The problem comes when we expect our relationships to be convenient. That's not realistic. Relationships aren't a matter of convenience.**

For relationships of any kind, you have to go back to the basics. Whatever happened to meeting a guy in the grocery store? What happened to meeting someone and saying, "Hi, I'm Jenny. How are you?" We've lost our sense of why that's important. Maybe you're wondering about that—why should you say hi to the guy in the grocery store when you have four online dating apps on your phone already? You can just find a guy there. In person-to-person encounters, you're always attracting and being attracted to the energy that will nourish your spirit. There's a reason that guy turned your head while you were walking down aisle seven, and it wasn't just that he was buying the same kind of peanut butter as you (although that's a great way to strike up a conversation!). Your energy was attracted to his energy.

You know that feeling, don't you? You meet someone for the first time or see someone who looks good to you, and you can't help but smile and blush a little. That's because your energies are communicating with each other and telling you both to pay attention to each other. When you're near someone, whether you're sitting next to each other or passing in the aisle of the grocery store or even sitting at a red light in adjacent cars, you can feel the energy from each other. You can feel the heat from each other's bodies; you can feel the vibrations running through another person, and you can tell whether your energies are in sync with each other. You're tapping into the electromagnetic energy of the universe when that happens.

If you think, *Yeah, she's cute, but if I want a girl I'll just go find myself one online,* you're going to miss out on what could be a real soul connection. You're ignoring your gut instinct and further disconnecting from yourself and finding your true love in this life. This doesn't mean I'm against online dating, however (see Chapter 6 for the *right* way to use online dating sites).

When Is Enough Enough?

Ask yourself a few simple questions:

- Do you text someone more than you talk to him or her?
- Do you take time to tell people you appreciate them?
- Do you tell them in person or by texting?
- Do you use your voice and not your hands to express love to someone?
- Do you verbalize your feelings to people?

That's it—just those five simple questions. Think about your answers. Are you talking to people? Are you truly connecting with them? Be honest with yourself when you answer, because if you're not honest, then I can't help you get your head out of your apps and find your soul connection.

We don't go from first grade into college. We go through first, second, third grade—all of elementary school, all of middle school, and all of high school, *then* we go to college. Everything we do is learning; we are like sponges. In the same way that you have to go all the way through twelfth grade before you get to college, you have to go all the way through yourself in order to connect. We're all here for a temporary human experience in which we are *meant* to connect. You need to be using your own psychic ability to connect with yourself so that you can be more connected with another person. And you have to stop looking at the edited version of the person.

> We're all here for a temporary human experience in which we are *meant* to connect.

Someone told me recently that you have to read more than one chapter to know whether you actually like a book—you have to give it a chance. It's the same with people, and it's the same with yourself. You have to stop editing yourself, stop giving people the chance to edit themselves, and really dive into the content that's between the covers of the book of someone. There's infinite energy inside a person and inside the book of that person. Go ahead and get lost in yourself for a while and see what you find.

You have to ask yourself the following questions: When is enough enough? When should I stop texting? Why shouldn't I text? Maybe you're even texting while you read this. Put the phone away and ask yourself more questions: Do I really want someone to appreciate me for who I am? Do I want to be loved? Do I want to be deeply connected to someone? Am I really ready for love?

If you are, then come with me on this journey, because I have written this book for you, to teach you how to connect with yourself and your energy and sift through all the Mr. or Ms.

Wrongs to find Mr. or Ms. Right. This is not just about your connection with the other person; it's about your connection with yourself. If you're not connected with your own darn self, you will be sitting on a rock for ninety years by yourself and never get to be with Mr. or Ms. Right.

Spiritual Baggage

How do you do this? How do you connect with yourself? You begin by understanding what spiritual baggage is and how it hinders you. Spiritual baggage is the emotions that you won't let go of. If you don't let go of this baggage, you won't be able to get clear. The baggage might come from childhood—how you were raised—or even just your nature. You may be an empath, someone who physically feels what other people are feeling, so you tend to carry around more emotions. You may think you're ready for love and a relationship, but you're actually not because you're still holding on to all that junk. And it is heavy. Maybe you find that you don't feel healthy or happy and that it's hard for you to feel grounded, focused, and positive. You're going to have to detox all that negative energy you're holding on to; you're going to have to take a spiritual enema.

The Cure for Spiritual Baggage:
The Spiritual Enema

You're going to have to bring all the crap that you've dealt with since the beginning of your life and relive it emotionally. Write down everything from your childhood, as far back as you can remember, until the present day. Remember how it all made you feel. Then you have to own it. You have to go deep into your core and identify where you're going, figure out where you belong, and understand that you are here to learn.

It's time now, as you're writing these things down, to stop being the victim in these situations and stop analyzing them. If you were hurt as a child by someone older than you in a position of authority, forgive that person. If you hurt others as a child and they in return hurt you, own that you hurt them first. Forgive them for their actions, and forgive yourself for hurting them. Go through every single detail of pain, own your role, and grant forgiveness. You have to get yourself to a higher level.

Even if your childhood was great, you have to explore these layers of your life to find your core. Everyone experiences pain. Go through your layers and admit to yourself, "I've learned my lesson through this." The process of the spiritual enema is not about sitting down and boohooing through all the crap you've been through. It's about you owning your role in this life, letting the pain go, and moving on. You have to sit quietly with yourself (turn off all your electronics!) and your pad of paper or journal and really focus on this if you want to be able to move forward with your life.

All of this modern technology is great to a certain degree. But at the end of the day, you should not try to live your life through an app, because you will never be able to; that's not really living. You have to get back to the basics: Who am I? Where am I? Where do I belong? How can I find the root of myself and connect to my soul?

Are you ready to get to work?

Chapter 2

Creating Healthier Relationship Patterns: The Story of Camilla and Michael

There is one thing that comes up over and over in my work: unhealthy relationships. Sometimes I'm working with clients who are currently in an unhealthy relationship, sometimes they have one in their past, and sometimes I watch them enter one, or even many, until they're ready to make changes. I've noticed that it's hard for people to realize that they're in one or that they have one in their past. My clients think that they have such a strong electromagnetic field with another person. They think they have such passion, but is it really passion or just lust? Is it an addiction? That's for them to determine.

It's important for people to learn how to go through an unhealthy relationship and get rid of it. You may think you're ready for a new life and a new relationship, but are you really? I asked one of my clients, Camilla, to share her story with us. Camilla is in a relationship that I call Sometimers. Sometimes she only wants to remember the good parts and not the bad parts. Sometimes she *chooses* to forget the bad parts. She wants love so badly that she's just settling and connecting to her lust for a man named Michael. It's important for Camilla to learn how to decipher what's healthy from what's unhealthy, and it's important for you, too. You can't go through life blindfolded.

Throughout this chapter, you'll find that the headings may help you identify whether you're in an abusive relationship or have been in one in the past. The information contained in each section will give you just one person's story of how that reality played out in her life.

I asked Camilla the other day to tell me what things were like in the beginning of her relationship with Michael. Here's what she said:

> It was a soul connection that caught me completely off guard. I was jolted by the connection. It's hard to describe, really, other than to say that I felt like I had known him for lifetimes. In the first two days of knowing him I felt like I had known him many times before. I had never slept with someone right after meeting them before, but I slept with him the first day after meeting him. I felt like God was in the room with us that night. In the beginning, we had a terrific, incredible, poetic relationship where everything was genuine, sincere, and kind. I fell in love without falling in love with him. Instead, it was like I had always loved him and was remembering him again. It felt like it had no boundaries: within one month I never wanted him to call me his girlfriend or marry me because labeling it would destroy it.

Camilla and Michael were married a few months after meeting each other. She had been living in South Florida with her family, and he was living in North Carolina finishing up school. Before they were married, she left her family and moved with him to the Pacific Northwest for a job. When the time frame on that job was up, Michael decided that Camilla should leave her job and they should move to another state. So they did. Camilla established herself with a well-paying job at a large company. They got married, and Camilla supported Michael while he wrote a novel. When he decided he wanted to be with his family in New England, they moved again, with Camilla again leaving her job and her life there.

A few months into their marriage, Michael cheated on Camilla. They tried very hard to work things out: they saw a marriage counselor, and Camilla alone began to make the changes they had discussed in counseling. Despite her efforts, they chose to enter a trial separation. Camilla moved back home to South Florida, and Michael stayed in New England with his family. They've been separated now for almost six months and have not seen each other since Camilla moved to Florida.

For the last six months Michael has been vacillating on whether he wants to get a divorce. Sometimes he lays down the law with Camilla and says this is absolutely what they must do. At other times he says he needs to keep his life with her. But even when he says that, they still never talk about moving back in together.

You Can't Cut Ties with the Person

Camilla and I have been working together for a while now to clear Michael's energy out of her. A week ago I told her to cut all communication with him so that she could focus on herself and sort out what she really wants. After a week she came in and told me she hadn't been able to do that. She had texted him to tell him everything negative that was going on inside her—that he holds her down, that he doesn't love her, that he hurts her—and she told him she was going to file for divorce. Two days later he told her he wanted to be with her. They talked for a few days, very sweetly, about the past and the beautiful parts of it. Camilla said she wanted to talk to him about the fact that he hit her and that he cheated on her. He responded by saying that the past is in the past and that's where it should stay.

When Camilla next came to see me, she told me that she was nervous. She thought that she had let me down by talking to him, that she had betrayed me. For the last few days she hadn't been doing the guided meditations that I'd recommended to her. She also hadn't been exercising or engaging with her creative side.

I told her, "You're betraying *yourself.* If you spend money to see a nutritionist because you want to lose weight and she tells you what to eat and what exercises to do, and then you eat a package of macaroons and don't exercise, did you betray her? No, you betrayed yourself."

Camilla understood that and agreed. She told me that Michael had come back, though. He wants to have her in his life now. I asked her why she thought that was, and she told me that she had informed him that she was going to file for divorce—that he wants her only when she pushes him away.

Camilla is completely correct. I told her, "He came back to you only because he's a bloodsucking vampire. This is how he got you in the beginning. He makes you feel vulnerable and insecure, like you have no confidence, like you can't live without him. Of course he wants you now. You're right. He wants you when he thinks he can't have you."

I asked her what she thought would happen if they got back together. She told me she thought it would be the same thing, because he refuses to talk about the things that hurt her. She's right. So why do it?

For Camilla, abandoning Michael would be like abandoning her child. Let's say she has a son who is jumping on the bed and destroying everything in the house. If he falls off the bed and breaks his arm, would she take him to the hospital or just leave him to cry? Of course she would take him to the hospital! What parent wouldn't? So I told Camilla that she has to ask herself, "Am I his friend, his wife, or his mother?" She knew the answer before I even asked the question; she is all three because he is weak and insecure.

Camilla is in an abusive relationship. This doesn't mean that she is getting hit every day. Abusive relationships can take many forms: the abuse can be physical, sexual, emotional, or mental. Camilla acknowledges that her relationship primarily involves the last two types of abusive.

I shared this with her: "I want you to be happy whether you're with him or without him. You have to be on the outside of this looking in. This is your life. This is your soul. No one knows the pain you're going through. You feel like you're investing in this to find your center, but the one who is getting hurt is you. You feel scared that you'll let everyone else down if he doesn't change, and I know you really want him to change."

You're Hooked on the Person

None of this is to say that Camilla doesn't love Michael or that she isn't *in* love with him; she certainly is. But he was never the person she fell in love with; she fell in love with a soul, not a person. So her work now is to detach herself from his soul. She has to pull away.

Camilla voiced something I've heard hundreds of other men and women say:

> I need something from him. I need him to call. I need
> to know that he's not going to leave again. That's all he's
> done these last few months—leave. The last few days,
> I could even tell that him being back was just another

part of the cycle of our codependent relationship. I was very calm and cautious while we talked. Then yesterday I didn't hear from him and I needed him. So I texted him this morning and let him know that I was missing him. He said he got wrapped up in his writing yesterday. I told him that maybe in the future we could just text each other before bed because it warms my heart to hear from him. Ten hours later, I still haven't heard from him. I've noticed that when he gives me attention I don't need it, but when he stops giving me attention, that's when I get upset. I had a rough day and felt really tired and really bad because I hadn't heard from him.

Camilla is addicted to her relationship with Michael. She is a strong, confident woman who usually owns her power. Since we'd begun working together, she had been able to clear her mind much more. But once she had gotten back into communication with Michael, he began sucking the energy out of her. Camilla described it this way: "It's like right now, this whole week, we've just been taking a breather. We've had a little bit of communication, and it's been sweet; neither of us has been controlling or possessive. We're just taking in the niceness before it blows back up again."

Michael, like most manipulative individuals, is very intelligent, which is part of what makes him attractive to Camilla. He knows what buttons to push. He knows he has to talk sweetly to her, and he calculates when to be nice to her. He knows he has to lure her back in so that she'll let her guard down with him and start trusting him again, so that he can push her away again.

Camilla reported that this cycle repeats for them every few weeks. Until now, the cycle took longer to complete, so it was harder for her to realize what was happening. She shared that she doesn't think she'll ever be able to get rid of him—that even in their next lifetimes they may come back as siblings because they are connected in such a way that no matter what happens, they'll always be joined. "I don't feel like it's ever going to really be over with him," she said. "That's just a temporary thing, to say it's over. I'm not saying it'll never be over in this lifetime. I feel like we may not make it through this lifetime, but in the next one we'll do it again. We may get divorced in a few months. Who knows?"

There's No Balance

I asked Camilla what she believed Michael brought to the relationship. She named a few things that he used to bring— emotional support, clarity, and insight—but added that now she doesn't get those things from him. When I asked her what he brings to the relationship financially, she said nothing. She pays for things because he can't afford to, even though he *can* afford subscriptions to dating sites and drinks at a bar. Camilla is choosing to nurture and take care of a man who is mentally and emotionally abusive and who can be physically abusive as well, and she knows it. Perhaps you have found yourself doing the same thing for someone and not getting the things you used to get in return.

You have to work on getting stronger. You have to use the *I am*: "I am light. I am love." Say it to yourself over and over. It's not that you're better than he is. It's that you're strong enough to do what you need to do for yourself, and you're not going to let one person pull you down. There will be many people in your life who will try to destroy and distort you, but the more that people try to bring you down, the stronger you will become. You have already realized that you are getting stronger. Now you have to put your big-girl panties on and fight through this. Only you can fight through it—that's why you have to do it. I get that you don't want to abandon him because you feel sorry for him, but you have to let him go so he can learn.

That's the truth, people. Whether you are currently in an unhealthy relationship or were in one in the past, you have to let the person go to learn on his or her own. You have to let other people go through their own things. They may want you to be there and emotionally coach them and help them. They may say they want to go back to the way things were. But you can't do that. You've sacrificed enough for a person who was or is taking advantage of you and not giving to you or appreciating you.

You Get Physically Sick

Being in an unhealthy relationship can suck your energy dry. When you're together you feel extremely high, and when you're not together you feel extremely low. Michael sucks Camilla's energy dry; he depletes her of everything and makes her want to scream. Everything she's holding on to is related to fear. She has a fear of failure and a fear of being alone. So to avoid failing at her marriage and to avoid being alone, she has given this relationship 100 percent while Michael has given 10 percent.

When I asked her how she feels being around somebody who just takes and takes and takes, here's how she responded: "For the last few days I have been sick. Like, physically sick. I can't stop throwing up, and I can't stop sleeping. I'm just sick. I thought it was what I ate, but I know it's him. I'm just sick over all of this stuff."

I told Camilla, "You're my client and I'm worried about you. I'm worried about your mind and your soul. I'm worried about you crashing and burning. You were finally getting your head above water; you were making your life your own again. But now you're caught in his web: you're damned if you do and damned if you don't."

You Sacrifice, Sacrifice, and Sacrifice

Camilla stopped me there and said exactly what I wish all my clients in this situation would realize: "I'm sacrificing what's best for me just to be with him." She could not have explained it better. She is sacrificing what's best for her—her physical and emotional health and the things she does to maintain that—just to be with someone who is sure only some of the time that he wants to be with her.

She said, "Here's the thing: There's no commitment from him about our marriage. There's no concept of him being in this state. I have no idea what he's doing or who he's spending his time with right now. When I told him I was filing for divorce, he said he wasn't going to sign [the papers]." I asked her why she was going to do that. She told me she's sick of going back and forth and back and forth and of him always changing his mind. He said that he wants to take things slow and see what happens. That's when she went off on him.

I asked her how she feels when she tells him to leave her alone and go away. At first she said scared; then she said proud. It's normal to feel more than one emotion at a time in any situation, and in this kind of relationship those two emotions coincide a lot. I told Camilla that Michael psychically feels when she's pulling away from him. She shared that Michael is a very spiritual man; that everything she's learned about energy and the spirit she learned from him. She also told me that he got drunk one night and said, "I am the universe. I am so much better than anyone."

I explained to her that he's at a higher vibration than the rest of us. He came here to learn, as we all do. In the physical sense he's human, but in the spiritual sense, because he is at a higher frequency than the rest of us, he can't live in the world the way everyone else does. He's still living a past life. He doesn't know who he is right now. He's trying to live in this world—this temporary human experience—and he's trying to connect with Camilla, but he can't because he can't even connect with his current self.

I do think that Michael loves Camilla, but in this case love isn't enough. Their souls aren't meant to be together this time. It's not that he doesn't have faith in their relationship or that she doesn't; I think they both do. It's just that they're both emotionally disconnected from themselves right now.

I compared the situation to getting shocked by static electricity. You feel a tremor as it goes through you. That's what Michael does to Camilla—he shocks her. I told her she has to be strong enough to not call him or text him. She has to switch from saying, "I love you" and "I care about you" to "I love you enough to let you go" and "I let you go into the universe, and I hope peace finds you."

Is This Relationship
Your Past or Your Present?

I asked Camilla where she thought this relationship with Michael came from and why she keeps repeating this pattern in her life. She told me that she thought it came from a past life. That may be true, but it came from right here as well. Camilla has a very trying relationship with her parents. They were very strict and controlling with her, and they often were a little more than just firm in disciplining her.

It's kind of like a preacher's daughter who grows up to be either a preacher or a stripper—one extreme or the other. Her environment was so strict, and she was always told not to do this or that. so she rebelled 180 degrees. The worst thing you can do is tell people not to do something; it just makes them want to go do it.

Camilla wants to break out of her relationship with her parents, and this is part of how she does it. This is where she's at. She has to work through these layers. She told me that she was willing to open up and start trusting herself. But she wasn't completely ready to leave Michael and let him be free; she was still hoping that he'd change. She wanted to know how I could be sure that he's not making any changes.

I told her that I was reading him through her energy. "If he was making changes, I could tell you. He's blocking you. He's saying he wants to talk and hang out because he's alone again. You're in a typhoon right now, and it's going around and around and will eventually suck you in. You won't be able to get out, and before you know it, it's going to be over your head and you're going to drown. How do I know he's not making changes? You said it yourself. You have to pull away. Do you know how many people live in relationships like this?"

Camilla replied, "A lot." She's right. A lot of people live in relationships like this, because people get used to things. For instance, someone who is being abused, like Camilla, may not even know how *not* to be abused. It becomes familiar and almost feels safe. I've had many clients who have been abused in many different ways. They choose to stay in that type of relationship, usually because they were raised that way.

It's similar to being raised by an addict: as an adult, you keep getting into relationships with addicts. You get in those relationships and adapt to what you grew up with. Even though it hurts, it sort of feels comfortable because it's what you've always known.

I told Camilla that if Michael hadn't pushed her away, she wouldn't be here right now; she wouldn't have moved to South Florida, and she wouldn't have come to see me. *She* didn't push *him* away. *He* pushed *her* away, and she let him because she doesn't know anything different at this point—he's been pushing and pulling at her the whole time. I told her to forgive him, to pray for him, and to begin talking about their relationship in the past tense. If she continues to talk about it in the present tense, she won't be training her brain to move forward from this.

You Think About Letting Go but Don't

I told Camilla, "If you're with Michael, you're not letting him go through his emotions alone. You're enabling him—you're keeping him from what he has to learn. It's like the seed of a rosebush: you plant it, you see the roses bloom, and then the roses die. This occurs so that a new rose can come along. This is part of your blooming. You're blocking the next person from coming into your life." I asked her how that made her feel, and this is what she said:

> When I think about it, this has all been strange. The first time I came to you, you told me that I had a soul mate coming and that he had dark hair. I've always been instinctively attracted to men with dark hair. [Michael is blond.] So I know that's not a coincidence. Nothing's a coincidence to me. Michael isn't my soul mate. We have a soul connection, but he's not my twin flame. As soon as I figured that out and learned that I would meet my twin flame in this life, it made me motivated but in a different way. I don't want to let go of this person I love so much

so that I can be with the twin flame. I married Michael, and I want it to work. But when I think about the next rose—when I think about my twin flame—I think of it as motivation to let this rose die.

I told Camilla that she was right, that it is good to think of it that way. She doesn't need to jump into a relationship with the next dark-haired man she meets. She needs to let the rose die so that she can work on herself. When we find a person like Michael, we hold on to him and wait for him to change; we keep praying and hoping. If someone is meant to be with you, then, yes, wait. But given how Michael is hurting Camilla, it's clear that he's not meant to be with her.

I told her she has to let go of him. This rose is the one she should *want* to let go, that she should *want* to be gone. I said that to her with great love, because if she doesn't find the love in herself, no one else ever will. She's letting Michael bully her and pull her down, away from herself.

Life is like a maze. It's not going to be the same thing every day. Maybe five to seven years ago Camilla could have said, "There's no way I would be in a relationship like this. That's not me, because I'm a problem solver." There is a difference between helping someone who wants help and nurturing someone who doesn't want to change. People aren't problems; they're people. Michael doesn't want to change. He has to be free and find himself. Then things will be better for Camilla.

You're Staying with the Person Out of Pride

The reality is that if Camilla doesn't leave her husband, she'll never have a chance of meeting her twin flame. If she keeps obsessing over Michael, she'll end up finding that she waited for him her whole life. She'll be seventy years old and we'll still be having this conversation. The only way to get out of his web is to cut all her ties to him. She can't do it little by little. That's not how it works. She can't call him, and she can't take his calls. She has to commit to that and follow through with it. She should file for a divorce, but she said that she wasn't going to yet because she wasn't ready—despite the fact that for almost a year the two of them had been taking turns saying that they were going to file.

Camilla said, "If he had any idea that I was going to leave him—I said I was going to file, and he said 'Go file. I don't freaking care.' The next day it was 'I love you.' And every day after that it was 'I love you.' A few days after the first 'I love you,' we ended up having a three-hour conversation because of how different he was. It worked. He pulled me in again because I don't want to be the one who screws up."

I let Camilla sit with that idea for a while. This is one of the main reasons people stay in relationships like this, so I thought it was important for her to think about it. People don't want to be "the one who screwed up." I think you have to really ask yourself: Screwed up what? Screwed up a relationship with someone who doesn't care about you? Screwed up a relationship in which someone hurts you or you both hurt each other? It's already screwed up, so be done with it.

When Camilla was ready, I asked her where she thought she'd gone wrong. She replied, "We tried to make it last forever. It would have been just as beautiful if we had been together and then let it go."

When Camilla met Michael, she was at a low place in her life. He came and rescued her as though he were the stars and the moon on a silver platter. It was as if there were nothing between the two of them; they were two people with one complete energy. They looked into each other's souls and let their walls down quickly because he had come to her when she needed him and she had come to him when he needed her. She was ready to give up on life because she didn't feel loved and accepted. He gave her everything she needed; he didn't judge her. But he used that same energy to manipulate her.

I see this all the time, and it can be a hard pattern to break. You may have noticed that Camilla repeated a lot of the same things and that she changed the subject when I asked her questions that had tough answers. Maybe you find that you have done the same in your current or past relationships. I believed it was important to point out because it is one of the hallmarks of an abusive relationship: your thinking gets circular, and you make excuses for your partner.

I want to tell you the same thing I told Camilla: You were there to help that person grow and to help yourself grow. Michael didn't mean to test or manipulate Camilla; he just did. At that point in the other person's life, you knew that you could help get him to where he wanted to be. You did that a lot for him—you built him up. You're still doing it. You're still supporting him right now. You seem to feel responsible for him. You have given up your happiness for him, and you don't want to walk away because you think he'll give that happiness back to you. You want to fight through it to be with him, but this is a relationship you have to let go of. And then you have to work on, and keep working on, you.

The Healing Process

Camilla was finally able to let go of Michael. I asked her to share what she found most helpful in the process of letting Michael go. Here's what she said:

> The thing that was the most helpful to me was crystal
> meditation therapy. I wear crystals constantly now to
> soothe my spirit and give me hope. Deborah gave me a
> quartz crystal. I put all of my negative husband energy
> into it. As I was meditating, I held the crystal in my hand
> and felt the negative energy of Michael come from my

center and go down through my arm, and I put it into the crystal. The crystal became a vessel for all those bad feelings so that I didn't have to hold on to them anymore. When I felt done emptying out that energy, Deborah threw it into the ocean, far away from me, so that the energy could not come back into me.

Now I try a different practice. I have purchased some crystals that carry healing energy—I particularly like rose quartz since it helps to balance the emotional highs and lows I used to feel. I hold the crystal in my right hand and feel the positive energy coming in from the crystal, up my arm and into my heart. This kind of meditation, where I am able to focus on a tangible object, worked especially well for me.

My meditations were aided by Deborah. She gave me recorded copies of her guided meditations. I listened to them every day. I think that it can be difficult, when you're first learning to meditate, to figure out how to not be distracted without instruction. So being able to take her home with me and focus on myself, in my own space, really speeded up the rate of my healing. It also really changed the way I think about the space I live in.

One of the most major changes I made that led to me healing was the process of setting up my own safe space. The room Deborah works in is a really spiritually clean space filled with a lot of cultural and spiritual amulets.

Going in there, I always automatically felt better. I began to wonder why I was choosing to live in a space that didn't make me feel the same way. She encouraged me to make changes in my space, and she gave me the motivation and creative inspiration to make my own space sacred and healing.

I brought in items that naturally have a high vibration on their own: crystals, plants, Himalayan salt lamps, incense, and candles—things that are natural or made of natural materials. I made a conscious effort to use natural light instead of artificial light and to keep my windows open so that the fresh air could come in. I feel very comfortable in this space. It heals me to come home and live surrounded by high-vibration objects. I find that I am more capable of continuing to release negative energy on my own, which helps me to stay balanced.

The change it has made in my life is undeniable. It's not that I don't still carry feelings about Michael. I believe I will always love him, but now I am better able to remind myself that I am a strong enough person to walk away, and strong enough to heal myself after pain.

Camilla is now ready to file for divorce.

Chapter 3

Setting a Goal: Finding a Soul Mate

You know how you're told that if you want to lose weight, you have to start small? Set yourself a ten-pound goal even if you eventually want to lose fifty pounds. Success is all about goal setting. If you're reading this book, I'm guessing that your goal is to clear yourself out in order to find a soul mate. People use the term *soul mate* a lot to describe a lot of different things; you may have even heard the term *twin flame* added on to it. Let's clarify so that you can understand what kind of goal you're setting.

Attraction comes in three different forms: psychic, physical, and a combination of the two. Which type of attraction you have with the person you're dating can be determined only by you. Your friends and family members can say whatever they want about the one you're with, but you have to really listen to your gut, and no one else, to determine what type of match you have.

The Physical Match

Have you ever met someone that you think is smoking hot? I know I have. Have you ever discovered that once you get to know these smoking hot types, you still use only that phrase to describe them, instead of *funny, sweet, interesting,* or *smart*? It turns out that there was nothing else there for you except how externally attractive these individuals were—maybe because they hadn't taken down their walls yet, or maybe just because you simply had nothing in common. That's kind of what it's like with a physical match: you find each other really attractive, but it ends there.

Now that's not necessarily a bad thing. Physical matches are great for a no-strings-attached hookup. So if you're looking for that, you've found the person for it. But understand that it will only ever be a hookup. Don't think you'll be able to marry the person. It doesn't matter how hard you try to make it work or find this person interesting; it will not work.

Because we are not entirely spiritual beings and we also possess a body, it can sometimes be hard to distinguish the lust that is part of a physical match from a true spiritual connection. It isn't always as easy as having nothing in common. So let's discuss a few things to look for.

You Think About the Person Only When You're Together

If all you're interested in with people is their physical qualities, or the physical relationship you're having, when you call
them you won't actually be calling to see how they are. You'll
never really be asking them about themselves; you'll only be
asking whether they're available when you need them to be. You
may also notice that if they aren't available you probably won't
care what the reason is, because you're really just looking for
one thing with them. You're not even willing to put yourself in
alignment with what they're doing in their lives.

You're not making yourself available to want to be with these
people, consciously or unconsciously. They could be incredibly
good-looking and you may be thinking, *Why can't I see beyond
the physical aspect of this person? Why can't I go to the next level?*
It's because you're not allowing yourself or wanting to let yourself
be spiritually connected with these people. No matter how hard
you try to be interested in them, you won't be, because you're
not connecting with them on a psychic level. You're looking at
something you want that's different from what's actually there.

You Don't Laugh Together

If you find that nine times out of ten you're not laughing when
you're with someone but you still find this person attractive, you

probably have a physical match. When you're with people who make you feel happy just by being around you, you're going to be more prone to laughing—it will be much easier to think the things that they say are funny. But if you find yourself with someone with whom you're not laughing the majority of the time, you're with someone you're attracted to but not someone you're connected to.

The purely physical match has nothing to do with a spiritual or an energetic connection.

Remember, the purely physical match has nothing to do with a spiritual or an energetic connection. Understanding someone else's humor and having a similar sense of humor is one way that people connect on another level. If that's not present in your current relationship, then you're in a physical match, not a psychic match.

You Describe the Person Only as Hot, Sexy, or Attractive

When my clients first come to see me, 99 percent of my clients, when they first come in, say, "I want my Prince or Princess Charming," and then they describe him or her: dark-haired with green eyes; they want the future partner to look into their souls and feel a physical connection and desire them all the time. And I say, "What about the rest? What happens on the inside?" I don't match people on a physical level. I match them on a spiritual level.

I tell them, "Your way is no good, because if you were in a relationship, you wouldn't be here right now. What you're doing isn't working." When you're thinking about your match, you can't only visualize how a person will look with you or on his or her own. If you find yourself doing that when you're with someone, watch out!

When you're identifying your match based on how people look, and you can't describe them further than by how they dress, what kind of car they have, or how handsome or pretty they are, you're not looking at the inside. Think about how you tell your friends about the date you went on. Do you say, "She and I talked and talked for hours," or do you say, "She had legs that went on for days and wore this sexy little dress"?

When you can't actually communicate with each other and you aren't able to get past what people look like, you're either not into them or they are not allowing you to be connected to them. If there's an attraction but no connection, you're in a physical match with the person.

You Don't Feel a Spark

Have you or your friends ever said, "He is really nice, but there's just nothing there"? That's what I mean when I say you don't feel a spark. You may find this person to be the hottest thing since sliced bread, but you're just not feeling it, no matter how much you try to open up or what kinds of things you're doing to try to make it work. You have a physical match, and it won't ever be more than that.

I have a client named Miranda. She always used to go for the same kind of guys: buffed and well put together and slightly older than she is. She wanted a guy who looked good next to her, and many of them did. But they were never interested in the same things; they didn't have the same hobbies. The guys she kept going out with were adventurous—they wanted to go sky-diving and explore the world around them, whereas Miranda preferred to be at home painting or crocheting.

She was never able to connect with these men on a psychic level even though she tried all the things they liked doing. The problem was that she was drawn to certain things for certain reasons, and because she was dating men based on their physical qualities and nothing else, she wasn't able to get what her soul really needed.

You have to walk away from such a person, thinking, *Wow. We just really clicked.* If you've never had that feeling before in the dating realm, you may be able to identify it from other parts of your life: your career, your pets, or your friends. Connections happen in all different places. But if you don't feel that way about the person you're currently dating, then you're looking at a physical match, not a psychic one.

You Don't Go Out Together

When you have a physical match with people, you're not interested in who they are inside. One of the ways you can tell is that you're not interested in taking them to meet your friends or your family. You should feel proud of the people you're dating and want everyone else in your life to meet them. If you find yourself constantly too busy to actually do something with them, or you call them up to see how they're doing but don't actually want to hear about that, then you have a physical match with them.

You have to ask yourself whether you are actually interested in communicating with them. Do you find what they have to say boring or annoying? If so, you're not connecting with them on the inside. You have no common interest in each other, even though you may be trying to.

* * *

If any of the above describes how you're feeling or behaving in your current relationship, then you have a physical match, not a psychic one. But that's okay! You may not find your soul mate the first time you try. People come into our lives for a lot of different reasons. If you find that you keep being in physical matches, it may mean that you have closed your heart to love. You'll have to work your way through the issues discussed in

Chapter 2 again before you move on. I know that you've made it this far in the book because you're looking for something different, something that will endure. The next section describes what you want to look for.

The Psychic Match

Basically, a psychic match occurs when you're connecting with someone on a spiritual level, not just a physical one. This means that whether you're going through the worst time in your life or the best time in your life, you have someone who really understands you. You can have a true psychic match with a friend as well as with a lover. It's as though your energy is inseparable. Having a psychic match with someone means that you should keep this person in your life, because real psychic energy is exchanged between you.

But when you become connected to someone's energy and you begin to share a vibration with each other, what's happening on the outside stops mattering so much.

One of the most common things I hear from clients when they find a psychic match is that the person they're with is someone that they probably never would have chosen because that person isn't what they were looking for on the outside. But when you become connected to someone's energy and you begin to share a vibration with each other, what's happening on the outside stops mattering so much. The ease, comfort, safety, and understanding that you get from a psychic match overrides what the person looks like on the outside; the inside becomes what matters the most.

Your Energy Is in Sync

Think about when you first met the people with whom you've had a psychic match. Did you find them so easy to talk to that it was as though you'd known them forever? That's one way to know if your energy is in sync. If you find that you act as if you're reading each other's minds, that also means your energy is in sync. It means that your energy has become intertwined. This isn't something that you can force; it just happens naturally.

If you have a lot of things in common with the other person, this doesn't mean that you're just complementing each other. Having things in common is important because it means that you were drawn to the same things without even knowing each other. It means that you can connect on a deeper level because you each came to these things on your own. Our energy is drawn to certain activities based on how the energy develops, so liking the same things means that your energies will more easily connect.

You Feel Disconnected When You're Apart

If you find yourself feeling scared, lost, and empty when you've gone a few days without talking to the person you're dating, almost like the emptiness of mourning, you may have a psychic match. It's almost as if you get scared because you feel empty—sort of like when a car is out of gas: it'll move if you really push it, but mostly it just stands still. Even though you may not always get along great, you feel depressed when you're not together. You find that the things around you are no longer as engaging or exciting as they used to be. It's hard for you to get through your normal daily life because you're used to constantly connecting with that person's energy.

When you feel an actual physical pain in your gut because you miss someone so much, or your body is filled with an aching because you're apart, that is the difficult side of a true psychic connection.

Sometimes this can be a good thing. When you find a true psychic match, especially a very strong one, you may suddenly feel more whole than you did before (which sounds impossible until you feel it for yourself), and having that person be gone for a few days means that you get to realize how connected you are. Perhaps you'll discover that you took for granted how good that connection feels. And perhaps it will reaffirm for you what you had already been thinking: that you have a true psychic connection with this person.

The Person Has a Lot to Offer

When people have a lot to offer, this doesn't mean that they buy you everything you want or give you money—that's not particularly important. It means that you feel an incredible emotional connection that feeds your soul. This is different from someone doing something nice for you that feels good. Although that's a great thing, what I'm talking about is feeling that your spirit is renewed just by being in the person's presence.

When you are near such individuals—not just when you're next to them or touching them but even when you're just in the same room—you feel at peace. Your soul is being fed with good stuff. You're so energetically connected that you're being nourished by the other person's positive energy. That's what it means for people to have something to offer. They offer your spirit something that other people can't or don't, and they don't do it consciously. Your energies are just that well in line.

You Don't Feel Alone Anymore

Even though you might not always get along so well and things go up and down, you believe there's nothing that you can't do as long as you have each other. You always know you are there for each other when needed. Even if you're far apart, you can still feel each other. It will be a different, somewhat disconnected feeling, but you'll still feel more complete than you did before you entered the relationship.

I met a couple recently that has been married for almost forty years—two-thirds of the wife's life and almost half of the husband's life. Both of them have lost their parents, they've built and lost and rebuilt businesses together, they've gotten jobs and lost jobs, and they've moved all over the world—not just to different states but to different countries, too. They also raised four children, all of whom were teenagers at the same time (can you imagine?). Here's what each one says about the marriage: "I'm pretty good on my own. But with my best friend here, we burn brighter."

That's what I'm talking about. You feel good on your own— you can handle a lot and take care of a lot; but with your match you could take on the whole world and be unstoppable. It is a true psychic match when your energy and purpose in life becomes much clearer because of the person you're with.

You Share Past Experiences

Suppose you were in a relationship in which your spouse cheated on you, and you meet someone who went through the same bad experience. You might be looking at that person and thinking, *He's too tall, and I'm too short. I'm going to look like a midget with the Jolly Green Giant.* But if you go deeper with that person and make a soul connection, it will be magnetic. Your energies were called to the same past experiences for a reason. That means your energies will line up well.

I once had a client who lost her soul mate and wouldn't let herself get past it. This happens in a lot of relationships: the one you thought would be your partner forever goes away and then you block yourself from being able to find someone else because you think that was your one true love. You have to actually learn how to defrost your frozen heart.

It's like going to an animal shelter and seeing a lovable puppy. You think that you should sleep on it before making a decision. In the morning you decide that the puppy is perfect for you, but when you go back, someone else has already adopted it. You get bummed out that the puppy is gone, and you go home. Meanwhile there are all those other puppies in the shelter that you aren't even seeing because you're bummed out. They need an owner and some love, too.

Some people come into your life for a temporary experience, and they have to leave so that a new experience can come. Don't shut yourself down because the only person you had loved up till now got away. You have to learn to open up your heart. Sharing past

Some people come into your life for a temporary experience, and they have to leave so that a new experience can come. Don't shut yourself down because the only person you had loved up till now got away.

experiences with someone means that your connection will be stronger, but it also means that you can teach each other how you've managed those experiences and how you've grown stronger from them. You never know what you can do for someone else unless you try. That process of teaching each other can make for a long-term partner or a long-term friend.

The Person Helps You Get Your Rhythm Back

You suddenly feel an energy inside yourself, as though you've been recharged. You were like a dead battery before this person came along, but now you feel alive again. That happens when you connect with someone even though you thought you could never love again because you were used and abused in the past. But now this new person gives you back the momentum that you need.

This is what I call helping you get your rhythm back. When a person comes into your life and something inside you shifts, you suddenly find that you're taking better care of yourself— maybe working out more or eating better. I'm not talking about an insecure person who decides to change in order to be with someone else. Something in the other person's energy just gets you all amped up and feeling the way you used to.

You Feel a Spark

When you feel butterflies in your stomach and can't take your eyes off the person; when you feel whole again, like the missing piece of your life has been found; and when you feel as if you've been with this person all your life even though it's only been ten minutes, that's what I call feeling a spark.

Do you find that when you're in a room with a bunch of other people, you can't see the other people, just your match? That's what I'm talking about. When you open up through your connection with that other person, your heart starts opening up—it may even literally skip a beat.

It's a deep, spiritual moment in your life that is very hard to describe. You will probably feel as though you're ready to burst. You may find yourself thinking that you've never felt this way before. You may even find yourself regularly excited to be around this person or even just to talk, because you're connecting on a much deeper level than you have ever connected with anyone else.

* * *

Finding a psychic match is a truly special thing, and it is something that you will know in your gut more than you'll be able to put into words. A feeling of certainty will come over you about your future and your present with that person that is unlike anything else you have ever felt. Then you'll know that you have a psychic match.

The Three Types of Soul Mates

It may sound strange to say that there are three types of soul mates. Shouldn't there be only one person who lines up with your soul? This is a common misconception. Many people have different kinds of soul connections with others. So let me help you differentiate between the types.

Soul Mate

A soul mate is someone you're obviously connected to, someone whose sentences you can finish. The sparks are so strong that when you're looking at each other, it's as if you're looking at each other's thoughts. The other person reads you, feels you, and connects with you.

You can have a soul mate and be connected, yet the relationship still might not work out. All that being soul mates means is that your souls had to meet in this lifetime. If you find a soul mate, try being with that person. Maybe you are supposed to be with that person to learn; maybe you are meant to bring a child into the world together. But just because your souls had to *meet* in this lifetime, it doesn't mean that your souls have to *stay together* in this lifetime.

Connecting Soul Mate

A connecting soul mate is someone you connect with on almost every level. This could be a great friend or a great partner. It is someone you will always be connected with—perhaps your best friend. No matter what happens or how much time goes by, you will always be connected to this person.

What makes the connecting soul mate different from a soul mate is that no matter how hard you try to be connected on a physical level, it won't work. It always stays in the friend zone, no matter how strong the connection feels.

Twin Flame Soul Mate

The twin flame soul mate is the hardest kind of soul mate to find and the hardest kind of relationship to maintain. Furthermore, you get only one in a lifetime. I know what you're thinking: *If it's the hardest to find, how will I ever find it? If there's only one, and there are nearly 7 billion people on this planet, I'm statistically out of luck.*

Stop that negative thinking! Don't be discouraged. Because soul mates are determined long before you're born, the energy of twin flame soul mates calls the individuals to each other. I know many people who found their twin flames quickly when they opened themselves up to advances in their jobs or to other things that were true to their core (such as moving to take care of a sick family member). It involves listening to yourself and trusting what you hear.

When you have found your twin flame, you will know it. It will be as if you have two physical bodies but are one connected soul: you feel a sense of pure completion. It's as though you have found the missing piece to a puzzle.

When you have found your twin flame, you will know it. It will be as if you have two physical bodies but are one connected soul: you feel a sense of pure completion.

The twin flame soul mate can be hard to figure out because the two of you are so much alike. You may always butt heads because you're so similar. But when you're with your twin flame, the connection is unlike anything you could possibly ever imagine; you're allowing that person to be completely inside you without having sexual intercourse. The connection is like fireworks. It may even make you feel sick to your stomach, but in a good way. You will think about the person no matter what, even ten or fifteen years later. You will actually be able to feel your twin flame thinking about you, and when you're thinking about your twin flame, you'll know it's because he or she is thinking about you.

When It's None of the Three

If you find yourself holding back from the person, if you're not being honest about how you feel, that's probably not someone you should be with. You should be able to tell your partner how you feel no matter what you're going through. You have to feel safe enough to let down your wall; if you don't, then you know that the other person is not a soul mate.

The Committee Will Guide You

There is a committee above us that watches us in everything we do. You can call the members of this committee angels, spirits, guides, teachers, whatever is most in line with your faith. Once you have gotten yourself out of your funk, taken your spiritual enema, and learned to communicate with other people and yourself again, you'll open up to trusting love for yourself; you'll start identifying the energy that's inside you. You'll feel heat in your body; you'll feel excited and may not even know why. You're teaching yourself to be connected on a psychic and spiritual level. You're becoming more advanced and grounded. The committee is watching you, even when you're not tuned in to yourself, but when you are you'll be able to hear the things they're guiding you to.

Suppose you're getting up to go to work. You pour a fresh cup of coffee and get in the car. As you're driving, you spill the cup of coffee all over yourself. You can't go to work covered with coffee stains, so you have to go back home to change. When you start driving back the way you came, you discover that there has been an accident. If the coffee hadn't spilled on you, you could have been part of that accident! I'm sure you've heard stories like this many times. There are so many of them because the universe will always guide you to where you need to be. You just have to trust your gut.

I had a client named Barb who had lived in Georgia all her life. She did the same thing every day: woke up, went to work by the same route, took the same route home, and did the same things once she was home. Barb felt stuck in a rut. She was getting close to forty and didn't know how to make a change in her life. I told her that if she didn't change, she would be alone forever. She kept feeling called to make a change, to move to Montana, but she didn't want to leave a secure job to go somewhere she'd never even visited before. Sound familiar?

A person who gets too comfortable doing the same thing every day will never have movement. It doesn't matter what you do in order to take a journey—sell your house or go on vacation—you have to take the journey. You have to be in a safe place within yourself, but you can't stay where nothing can touch you, like the place Barb was in. Your knight in shining armor is not just going to show up at your door. You have to be open to making changes, and you have to listen to the nagging feeling that's telling you to make a change. That nagging feeling is the committee guiding you to your soul mate.

Barb was finally able to quit her job and move to Montana, and she is now settled in a happy life there with her soul mate. By listening to her gut, Barb found the person that God wanted her to be with.

Just like Barb, you have to stop putting limits on yourself if you want to find the love of your life. You have to open yourself up to change and trust that the committee and God will guide you down the right path. You have to stop second-guessing yourself and what you're feeling in your gut. Remember, your gut is the committee's way of communicating with you. It knows what it's doing, so trust in what you're hearing.

Chapter 4

The Twin Flame: The Story of Danielle and Andrew

ll the information and descriptions in the world can't change the fact that no matter where you are in your life—whether you're in your early twenties and have never been on a date or you're in your late fifties and have lost your partner through death or divorce—it can be easy to lose hope that you'll find your twin flame soul mate. The thing you hear most often is that if there's only one twin flame for you, you'll never find him or her. I know I already told you to stop that negative thinking, but I realize it's not always that easy.

So I asked one of my clients, Danielle, to share her story. Like many of my clients, she had lost faith in love—then she found her twin flame. She is just one of many who have done the necessary work to find a soul connection that will last the rest of their lives. Her journey to find her partner, Andrew, was not an easy one, and she did lose faith at times along the way. But when she opened herself up to loving *herself*, her soul mate walked through the door.

The next section is Danielle's story in her own words.

My Journey

My husband and I have been together for almost eight years. I'm fifty-one and he's fifty-five. It was a long journey for both of us to find each other, but I can honestly say that I wouldn't change any part of my past, because it brought me to Andrew.

Andrew and I met through our children. Their paths crossed, and as parents of children do, he and I got to know each other because of our children. At the time I had been divorced for a few years and wasn't looking for anything romantic, mostly because I didn't believe that I deserved to have it.

Some people enter a state of chaos late in their lives; some people are born into it. I am the latter type. My father passed away when I was very young, so I was raised by a widow. I grew up in the Deep South without a strong male figure, and when I was sixteen I fell in love with a man. We moved to South Florida, where I still live, when I was eighteen because he had a job there, so I followed him and went to college.

My marriage wasn't safe, however. My husband disrespected me in extreme ways, both in private and in public. I kept thinking, *If I just change this thing about myself, I can make this relationship work.* There was something new to change about myself every few months, though. I was like a lot of people: I spent most of my time trying to be someone else so that other people would love me.

That was how I thought marriages worked. That was a hard time for me, filled with a lot of sadness. Some good things did come out of that sorrow, like my children, but I was sad most of the time. I just kept trying to make things work, but I couldn't see myself clearly enough to figure out how I could make them work, and neither could my husband. My own distortion of myself had allowed me to choose someone who was equally distorted, though in a different manner.

I decided to see Deborah after I had divorced and taken out a restraining order on my ex-husband. I wasn't looking to make another match anytime soon; I just knew that my spirit needed healing. I wasn't completely alone; I had friends, male and female, that I spent time with. But I was so depleted and dried up from my marriage that it took every bit of energy I had just to get up and do what I needed to do to be a good mother to my three children. They were my audience during everything I went through in my marriage and my divorce. Children have their own personal challenges and struggles as well. You can't save another person from drowning if you're drowning, too. My children were also in some measure of crisis, so I had to figure out how to hold myself together enough to be there for them. I had to heal my spirit.

Whom Can I Trust?

Deborah pointed out to me something that I think is true of a lot of people: "You trust the wrong people too much and the people you should trust not enough." She was right. I wasn't trusting anyone correctly. You should have faith in some and stricter boundaries with others, but I didn't have either. I was coming from a heartbroken background and making decisions based on heartbreak instead of love. I had to learn to love myself enough to trust my gut.

I'm a highly intuitive person, but I would go against what I knew in my gut. I started to doubt myself early in life, and that doubt only grew, to the point that I didn't even trust what was in the very center of myself. I could not figure out that I was the person I thought I might be. Instead I carried a lot of things inside myself that the world—my family, my teachers, and other people—told me. My perception of life was blurred by my past, and I needed to put on some spiritual glasses.

After my divorce, I realized that I had suffered my whole life from what I call buzzy brain. Stuff—any kind of stuff—just spins around in my head. I was keeping my brain busy so that my soul couldn't deal with things. I thought that if I could just keep thinking, then I wouldn't have to feel pain, or maybe I could think my way out of my emotions. I spent my time filling my brain up with staying busy until it was time to go to bed at night. That's not the way you heal your soul. I had to learn to be quiet and still. I had to calm my buzzy brain and be able to just say to myself, *This is it. This is where I am.*

Finding a Calm Place

As I was learning to calm myself down while emotionally and legally dealing with a divorce, trying to help my children, and juggling every piece of my life, a man kept popping up in my life: Andrew. Now I can look back on it with much more clarity and see how our souls were called to each other, but at the time I only understood that there was a kindred spirit in Andrew, that I felt a different kind of connection to him. I knew that he was acting happy but coming from a sad place, just as I was. I kept thinking, *Being with this guy might be awesome, but it's not for me.* I kept looking at the chaos around me—it was like a circus with monkeys and fire jugglers—and I thought, *I cannot bring someone else into this mess. He'll either create more chaos or I'll ruin him with mine.*

I went to Deborah because I was at a crucial point. I kept looking at the circus, and I didn't know whether I needed to cut Andrew loose or buckle my seat belt for the ride. She told me he was my twin flame soul mate. Looking back, I now realize I knew that in my gut, but I needed to have it told to me. Because of the things I'd been through, I kept saying to myself, *This can't be for me.* I talked myself out of everything positive, all the time, because I was so used to being disappointed. I was trying to discount Andrew with the chaos, but what I didn't realize was that the work I was doing on my spirit was taking effect: the chaos was abating and the circus tents were being packed up.

I knew what I wanted in a partner, in theory. I knew that I was looking for someone I could trust, with whom I could feel safe, because I had always felt unsafe. But I didn't know how to get to a safe place. I didn't even know what that might look like. It's kind of like this: If you had to identify E. coli, you probably couldn't. I am a scientist; I work with microbes. So if I said to you, "This is how you find this germ on this plate; here's what it looks like," you could do it then, under my guidance. I had to follow the way on which Deborah guided me in order to become able to understand how to find safety and peace and to understand that I had already found it in myself and in someone else. I know what it looks like now.

I finally decided to listen to my gut and my guide and trust myself: I decided to let Andrew in. I was shocked to discover that our backgrounds paralleled each other's. Our families and previous marriages had undeniable commonalities. We share the same kind of sadness, even. When you start to see that in someone else, you can say, "I know your sadness. I know your happiness, too." You can come to a different kind of understanding of the person, and he or she of you.

I know what Andrew's sadness is, and I am careful to cherish those things about him because I know how he feels. I don't look at my past and think that I wasted my whole life. I look at it and realize that my past brought me to him. I had to come through it the way I did so that when I stood in the presence of Andrew I could say, "Here you are, and here I am. I want to be the best I can be with you."

Unexpected Inspiration

My relationship with Andrew inspired me to look at the things I needed to heal in myself. I can honestly say that for the first time in my life I have a refuge in another person; I know that someone has my back. I just know it. It doesn't matter what's going on around me, I know that I am cherished—that I am both loved and protected. It doesn't mean it's perfect all the time or that we never fight. Of course we do; we're humans in a relationship. But a fight doesn't make me insecure anymore. We both work to resolve the underlying issue.

I always had doubts about myself in the past. I doubted what I was doing or whether I was in the right place. Even in my previous marriage I wasn't sure I was in the right place. I kept thinking, *It doesn't have to be this painful.* I was right. Andrew meets me where I'm at: I know that all I have to do is be the best me that I can be, and that person is the one he'll love. That always makes me want to work harder on myself and be able to stay at peace with myself.

It's hard to know what changed: Did I change my life, and now I get to be with Andrew? Or did Andrew change me? I think it's both. I was working on changing my life, on pushing negative energy out and inviting positive energy in, and I got to be with the largest source of positive energy I've ever experienced because of it. Before I would have thought, *I don't deserve this in my life.* I would have picked apart whomever until I found enough flaws to walk away from him, no matter how great he was—I was already trying to do that with Andrew when I first met him. Now I ask myself, *Why not me? Why not have faith?*

It used to be that being off center felt normal to me. Now, so many years later, being centered feels normal to me. I've been able to do enough work on myself to make a difference for myself, and the incredible benefit of doing that work is that I get to spend the rest of my life with my twin flame. There is something about our energies combined that creates a healing space for both of us.

Ultimately, it's my responsibility to do what has to be done. It was up to me to heal my own broken heart; it still is up to me to handle my own sorrow. It's up to Andrew to take care of his own grief as well. But when our energies come together, when we're in the same space or in contact with each other even just over the phone, there's something healing about that; it is a relief beyond measure to be in each other's presence.

Finding Balance

Some kind of special exchange happens between us, beyond the everyday "I'll do the laundry if you'll do the dishes." I am definitely the more spiritual person. Andrew tends to be highly analytical; he likes for there to be a plan and to understand every detail of each step along the way. I'm much more willing to fly by the seat of my pants, sometimes to my own detriment. What I've noticed between the two of us is that somewhere there's a balance. It's not just that he makes a plan while I don't have one; unintentionally I also started learning to be more structured while he has learned to be more loose.

I see a side of him now that, without a doubt, no one else has ever seen. Sometimes you are born into this world getting hurt by your parents and siblings and best friends. That's how it was for both of us. By the time we got together, we were both feeling the same pessimism: *That was all pretty rotten. Who's even left over that I might want to try to love?* Then we trusted our guts, and our whole worldview changed. We found the glasses that we knew we needed.

We're feeding off each other in a positive way now, and it is creating a balance inside each of us, separate from the balance in our relationship. I think that the more we learn and grow, the more that balance becomes evident to both of us. We all have bad days and tough days; we all get annoyed by something at work or feel down about the past. But now I find that I'm much more able to keep that all-encompassing negative energy from my past out of my present life.

What It's Like to Be Together

When I listen to people talk about what they're looking for in a relationship, or when I watch television shows and movies, I see an image that's created of the perfect marriage: there's no fighting, you go to fancy dinners and get nice jewelry, and you're adored. Or else it's the complete opposite: an arduous task of negotiation and sacrifice. I used to think that way. I used to think that relationships were always this combination of movie dinner scenes and impossibly difficult work. I was wrong.

This is not to say that my husband doesn't put his best foot forward in caring for me; he certainly does. But the joys of our partnership aren't in those overt gestures. They're in the diet soda he puts in the freezer for me so that it will be ice-cold when I get home from work. They're in the moments he loosens up and walks away from the dishes that have to be done so we can go to the beach instead. They're in the effort and energy that I *enjoy* putting into myself and into our relationship. It's not hard to be married to Andrew, the way the media tell you it's hard. Things sometimes get difficult, and we have to work through them. But it's not a battle. We take turns sustaining each other. There's peace here—serenity, growth, love, and light.

How I Opened Myself Up

I could not have gotten to this place without Deborah's teaching. I had to learn to quiet down my buzzy brain, and she helped me do that. I used to be unable to tolerate not having the TV or music on; now it's nice to have the silence. I had to actually practice that—I had to sit in silence with myself. It seems almost silly now to think that I could barely handle half an hour of silence a year ago; now I love it. It was incredible to discover that doing that allowed me to be open with myself and with others. I gained a better grasp on who I was because I wasn't constantly clouding up my mind with tasks and thoughts.

Before meeting Deborah and learning how to quiet my mind, I didn't see myself as particularly valuable. It's a funny thing: when you try to keep pain out by filling up your mind with other things, you keep the goodness out, too. I wasn't just guarding myself from feeling my internal pain; I was also guarding myself from feeling my internal love. I had to actually be reminded to do nice things for myself and allow myself to realize that I am good at what I do. I created affirmations for myself that allowed me to realize that I was worthy of being cherished. The more I told myself my positive qualities, and the more I made time to be good to myself through the things that I enjoy doing, the more I understood my value.

Understanding my value brought me to a point where I could be with someone who values me, who sees me as I am and loves the very core of my personhood. I am not just loved or adored; I am *cherished* by the man I am with. I never thought I would get to be with someone who cherishes me. I never thought that I would be able to find my twin flame soul mate, but I absolutely have.

Set aside your fear. Take a chance. Learn to trust what you know inside yourself. You will be amazed at the incredible places to which your life will take you and the deep joy you'll be able to experience.

* * *

What Danielle and Andrew have, you can have, too. But as she said, it took a lot of work to get her to the point at which she could truly let love in. She had to get herself out of her own head and start looking at life through a different lens. Now she gets to spend the rest of her life with her twin flame soul mate, knowing that she is cared for, loved, and cherished.

Four Good Reasons for Dating Guidelines

I have found, both in my work as a psychic and in my personal life, that when individuals understand the purpose behind something they're doing, they're much more likely to do that thing. Maybe you've found that to be true as well. I could give you all the dating rules in the world, but would you really follow them if I didn't explain why you should? I know I wouldn't. So let's take a look at four good reasons to set dating guidelines and stick to them.

Self-Respect

You have to respect yourself. I cannot say this enough. You have to respect yourself, or no one else will. By setting dating criteria, you're showing that you have high standards. By sticking to those criteria,

> You have to respect yourself, or no one else will.

you're showing that you will not settle for anything less than your high standards. However you approach a relationship from the beginning is how the relationship will evolve.

I had a client recently who was in a relationship with a guy who was really nice, intelligent, and very handsome. They didn't set or follow any dating criteria, however, so I told her that I thought the situation was going to be bad. She said, "Oh no, it's going great! We see each other every day. We're really happy!" But sure enough, two months later, I got a phone call from her saying, "He's just not into me anymore. He's not attracted to me anymore."

Do you know what that means? He didn't respect her because she didn't respect herself. As quickly as something starts is how quickly it can end. But if you set your standards high and demand that someone respect you, you will be able to sustain yourself through the relationship. I don't mean that you should yell at people and tell them what to do; that doesn't warrant respect from anyone. I mean that you must hold fast to your principles.

I had another client who thought the guy she was dating was really hot and cute and nice. I told her to remember the rule of three: go on at least three dates within three weeks, and always wait three months before you consummate the relationship (see Chapter 5). Someone who really wants a lasting relationship with you will agree to that. The client called me up after she and this hot guy had been together a while and said, "You were right. I followed the rule, and he walked away." I asked her, "Do you respect yourself for sticking to your convictions even though he left?" and she said, "*Absolutely*. I was able to leave the relationship without being used."

So, reason number one: *Set dating guidelines and stick to them because you respect and care about yourself.*

Deep Connection with Others

When you set dating guidelines and stick to them, you are able to present yourself more openly because you have something in place to remind you to be conscious of your behavior. If the guidelines are in place, you'll have to check yourself during the dating process. This will force you to slow down and pay better attention—not just to yourself but to your date as well. You will be able to connect more deeply with him or her because you're connecting with yourself.

By believing in the one you're with (yourself), you're going to make your dates feel comfortable. They'll think you're easy to talk to because you won't be talking so much about yourself. You'll be able to ask them about themselves more freely because you won't constantly be assessing them. You'll be able to connect with them more freely, too, because you are connected to your own energy. And when you do that, the sky is the limit!

Reason number two: *Set dating guidelines and stick to them because you want to connect with the person you're dating.*

Self-Worth

You have to know that you are good enough. If you go on a date thinking, *This person is too good, hot, sexy, pretty, or stylish [or whatever] for me*, you'll be sitting on a rock for the rest of your life. Even worse, if you go on a date thinking that you're not good enough for that person, you may come to believe that you can be with him only if you change things about yourself. Then you are no longer bringing your genuine self into the relationship, and you will find yourself endlessly thinking, *I need to make this person happy. I need to be good enough for him.*

Wrong!

You can't be in a relationship to please someone else. Nobody gets to manipulate you like that, and no one will unless you allow it. If you clear your mind and your spirit and open yourself up to being loved, then no one will be able to take advantage of you. You have to believe in what you feel. And you can do that only if you know deep in your soul that you are good enough.

Reason number three: *Set dating guidelines and stick to them because you are good enough, as you are, without changing.*

The Old Way Didn't Work

How long have you been in the dating field? How long have you been looking for love and striking out? How long have you been using the same old method to enter a relationship that never turns into a lifetime commitment? Did you ever stop to think that maybe you should change that method? It obviously sucks, because it's not working.

Reason number four: *Set these dating guidelines and stick to them because your way didn't work.*

* * *

Nine times out of ten, the people who follow these guidelines will end up with someone with whom they feel a soul connection, because these guidelines help you connect to the other person's pure energy. And nine times out of ten, people who don't follow these guidelines will end up in a physical relationship (rather than an emotional and physical relationship) that lasts for only a few months and is then over.

If you stick to these guidelines, you will get to know each other on a much deeper and spiritual level. Emotional relationships are much deeper and far stronger than any physical relationship ever could be—they are about two people having a trust and a bond with each other.

In my twenty years as a psychic, these guidelines have proved to be effective for my clients. So if I've been able to make thousands of matches through these methods, why couldn't you be another success story?

Chapter 5

The Rule of Three

Maybe you're beginning to wonder why a book that guides you to your twin flame soul mate is filled with do's and don'ts of dating. The truth is this: you may not find your twin flame soul mate on the first attempt. I know that's seriously ungratifying to hear, but the reality is that if you don't find the person, it's probably because *you* aren't ready to, and *you* need to work on you. It's kind of like finding your favorite restaurant: Is your favorite one the first one you ever went to? I'm going to guess not. Sometimes you have to test things out until you find the perfect one. But I promise you that if you follow the rules and the guidelines set forth in this book, you absolutely, without a doubt, will find the right person.

Although I believe that all of the information in this book is important, following the rule of three is *so* important that I decided it deserved its own chapter. The rule of three can be remembered this way: Three dates, three weeks, three months. *Always go on at least three dates with the person within three weeks. Always wait three months before you consummate the relationship.*

The reasons are simple. On the first date you're uncomfortable; you're just starting to get to know each other and feel each other's chemistry. On the second date you're starting to be more comfortable than you were on the first date, so you're able to interact and have more of a conversation. By the third date you can finally really tell whether there's chemistry between the two of you and if there's a connection as well.

If you're looking for a relationship that will actually last, having that chemistry and understanding each other's body language is important. If you're really looking to have a soul connection, you want to give each other three months without having your physical parts connect.

> **If you're looking for a relationship that will actually last, having that chemistry and understanding each other's body language is important.**

You're going to have to ask yourself, *Do I really want to put an effort into this?* By putting a three-month waiting period on the physical aspect of a relationship, you're saying something like "Here's a piece of delicious chocolate cake. But don't eat it." Immediately you want to eat it. When someone says, "Don't do this for three months," it's the same thing. And I know it's hard, because we're all human and have a physical need for one another. You just go right ahead and do what you have to do by yourself when you get home, but don't give in to your physical desire for the other person until the three months are up.

What Happens When
You Don't Wait

When you get something too quickly and too easily, you might react like *Eh! That wasn't even a struggle.* When you have something to fight for, you want it even more. So start out your new relationship by saying no. Go ahead and let the other person fight for it for a while. The more you say no, the more you don't allow the physical to control you. Saying no allows you to respect the physical. You get more time and energy to get to know the person you're with.

A relationship involves communication with each other. If you're physical with someone every day, that may be great. But let's get real: What do you do with the other twenty-three hours of the day? A whole heck of a lot! Don't you want someone who will be your companion for more than just one hour? Relationships break up because people stop talking to each other. You start living your life and getting further and further apart. Even the physical act may become a chore.

People figure, "If I don't give it up, then someone else will, and I won't get to have him or her." Maybe that's true: maybe that girl you think is so hot has a line of other guys or girls just waiting for her to be free once she's not into her current partner anymore. You know what, though? Walk away. That girl is just in love with herself, and you don't need that kind of egotistical energy around you; it'll only bring you down.

If people are not willing to follow the rule of three, then as quickly as the relationship started, no matter how strong a connection and vibration there may be, that's how quickly the relationship will end. Even though two people may have had a great chance to be together, they won't get to be, because the relationship will end before it had a chance to actually start.

Why We Don't Wait

I met with a client recently whom I'll call Marissa. She was in a relationship with a man, and she was telling me things like "I love this guy. I think he's the right guy. I can't get him out of my head." But he was actually a total loser. Marissa was changing her whole life for him. She moved to be with him, then he decided he didn't want to live there anymore. So she gave up her job and the proximity to her family and moved again. Then he dropped her for another woman while they were still together. She wants them to stay together, but it isn't going to happen because he's already with another woman!

What happens in these cases is that the guy knows what's going on and the girl does, too. But she has on rose-colored glasses. She knows that his glass is only half full, but she thinks she can change him and fill up his glass to make him happy so she can have a fairy-tale ending. Yet she's looking at something that's not real; she's looking at something that doesn't exist.

Marissa is looking at this guy and saying, "Hey! I need some TLC, too." But the reality is that he can't give it to her because he doesn't have it to give. So I told her, "You're going to be *that* stupid that you're not listening and loving with your heart? You're just opening your legs."

There were no dating rules at all in that relationship. They just jumped right into it and here they are, three years later, in the exact same place.

Just as in Marissa's relationship, people think that the physical relationship will make the other person want them more; they believe that it will bind them together. There is certainly a release when two people have sex, but following this rule is about being obedient to yourself. It's all about you. Just like the client who was able to see the person she was dating walk away without feeling as though she'd lost her self-respect, you'll be able to have the same feeling. If the person you're with is pressuring you to give in, just don't give in. You have to really ask yourself if the relationship is worth keeping. Is it really worth being in? If it is, the other person will respect you enough to listen to what you want.

What Happens When You Do Wait

Going on three dates with someone and waiting three months before having sex gives you time to create a more structured environment. You don't want to jump from the frying pan into the fire. You also don't want to become bored and lose interest. By waiting three months you get to say to yourself, "I've done a great job honoring this rule"; to your partner, "Thank you for respecting the rule I set"; and to each other, "I've returned—let's get to it!"

When this is the tone you set for your relationship, you're entering it with respect and maintaining that respect through-out the course of your early interactions. The way that you are in the beginning of the relationship sets the tone for the rest of the relationship. This isn't to say that if you're all starry-eyed and enamored and blind to the person you're with at first (because, like Marissa, you're simply in love with the idea of being in love) that you'll be that way throughout the relation-ship. As quickly as the fire is lit, that is how quickly it can be extinguished. But if the beginning of your relationship is about respecting each other, that respect will carry through the course of your relationship.

By setting the tone for things—by saying to the person you're dating, "I respect myself enough to try to enter a partnership"— if it's meant to be, the other person will respect that about you. If it's not meant to be, then you'll know pretty quickly. By doing this you are giving both of you the chance to realize you're not just using each other. This is why it works and has been so effective with my clients. If you can get through the first three months and really make it work, then you can last a lifetime.

The Filler Relationship

Sometimes you have to have what I call a filler relationship on your way to your soul mate. A filler relationship is someone you like to go out with and explore with, but you don't consider this person your soul mate. Sometimes it's better to do that—it can be better than sitting at home by yourself.

I don't mean that you should use such people only to have fun. Be clear with them that you don't see the relationship going somewhere but that you like their energy and the new things they expose you to. When you're looking for the perfect person, for your twin flame soul mate, sometimes you have to try new things in order to get to the right one.

You never know what you can learn from someone, and you really never know where a relationship could lead or to whom or what it could lead you. Let's say you meet someone who's really fun and exciting and wants to do things that you always wanted to do but couldn't figure out how to do by yourself, like fishing or ballroom dancing. This person could help you get to those places. Then maybe you'll meet your soul mate on a fishing trip or at a ballroom dancing class that you otherwise wouldn't have been attending.

Finding your soul mate doesn't happen when you most expect it; it always happens when you least expect it. I have had clients who found their soul

Finding your soul mate doesn't happen when you most expect it.

mate right away, clients who waited twenty years before meeting their soul mate, and clients who were married multiple times before finding their soul mate. You don't get to decide the timing of finding the person you feel the strongest electromagnetic attraction with. So you might as well have some fun and learn new things while you're looking!

You also never know: the person you aren't sure you feel a connection with but have tons of fun with might very well be your soul mate. Maybe *you* are the one putting up a wall and resisting being loved. There's a reason you're enjoying this person, and it could simply be all the things you're learning, but it could also be more. You won't know unless you try and go into trying with an open mind.

One of the reasons I advise against consummating a relationship until after the third month is that once you do that, you're bound to each other. If you can tell you're in a filler relationship and you bind yourself to someone else, you may meet your soul mate during that time and miss out on being with that person because you can't break the bond you've made with someone else.

I know it feels easy to walk away from someone you've had sex with, and maybe it was for you in the past. But which was it easy for you to walk away from: a one-night stand or a relationship? Walking away from the one-night stand was probably easy, but not walking away from the relationship. You bind yourself to someone you sleep with, and breaking that bond takes much longer than never having formed a bond at all. So keep yourself free from ties you don't need just yet and focus on having fun, learning new things, and loving the one you're with.

Chapter 6

The First Date: Tapping into the Other Person's Energy

S o you're feeling ready, right? You've taken the time with yourself to get to the point where you truly feel open to giving and receiving love, you've forgiven those in your past who have hurt you, you've taken up something creative, you've committed to the rule of three, and you've gotten your head out of your app. When you're ready for the first date with a new person (or a person you've known a long time), I have eight first-date reminders for you.

Slow Down

Take a deep breath—right now, before you go on the date, and while you're on the date. When you feel yourself getting caught up in this fast-paced world, take a deep breath. Everything in this world is go, go, go, and if you don't take a breather every now and then, you'll never be able to enjoy the finer things in life: taking a walk, writing things down, looking at the clouds. Those are *really* the finer things.

While you're on the first date, relax! Enjoy yourself! You're getting to meet someone new. I know that sounds easier said than done, but if you focus on really getting to know the other person, you'll soon forget that you're nervous. Ask lots and lots of questions about the person. Here are a few easy ones to get you started: What do you do for a living? What do you like to do? What are your hobbies?

When you make conversations about the people you're talking to, they get to talk about something they already know a lot about: themselves! That will help them feel more comfortable, which means that they'll ask you questions back. The more back-and-forth there is, the more comfortable you'll both feel, and before you know it you'll be having fun.

When you don't slow down and calm yourself down enough to focus on the other person, he or she will lose interest in you in a hurry. The most common complaint I hear from people about their dates is "They were only interested in themselves. They never asked any questions about what I like to do or what I do for a living."

Even a date who doesn't end up being *the one* can become a good friend.

Remember that you're learning from everything you do. Going out with someone else is about learning, just as anything else is. So have fun talking to each other. Even a date who doesn't end up being *the one* can become a good friend. Or that person may actually be great for someone else in your life.

A client I'll call Jimmy went on a date with a woman awhile ago. He thought she was really cool, but he just wasn't sure beyond that; he didn't feel that strong of a connection to her. She let him know that she was giving away a puppy because she was moving from a house to an apartment that didn't allow dogs. He didn't have a desire for a dog, so he let a friend of his know. His friend and the woman hit it off, started dating, and are now talking about getting married. You never know what may happen when you open yourself up.

Let Go of Expectations

Be open to whatever happens. If you go on the date thinking, "I'm just going to go out and have fun. I'm just going to see what happens"—just as you would if you were going out with one of your friends—and it works out, you'll have a lot to be thankful for. Never look at going on a date or having been on a date as "the date from hell." Just as with Jimmy, your "hell" may be someone else's heaven. Everything's a learning experience. If you project the image of "I hate the dating scene. Everybody sucks," then you're the one creating bad energy.

When you go out with someone for the first time, don't think, "Is he or she going to be right or wrong?" or "Am I going to be right or wrong?" Just go into it very calmly and be yourself. Don't let your anxiety kick you. You know how it is: you start obsessing, *Am I standing the right way? Do I look the right way?* When you walk into the place you are going to on the date, you may start to get anxious, sweat, and feel your heart flutter. Just exhale slowly. Relax, and pretend you're out with one of your best friends with whom you only expect to have fun.

I had a client named Julie who went out with a guy. She kept thinking things like "He's going to be perfect. He's going to be this and that, and our relationship is going to be great." They sat at a restaurant bar, and at that moment she thought he wasn't paying attention to her. She thought he was talking to everyone else and looking at everyone else. She felt completely ignored, yet he was totally into her!

The problem was that she had set her standards so high and was expecting some very specific things, so she began criticizing everything about him. In order to get her to look past that, I had to force her to rid herself of her expectations and go on a second date even though she didn't want to. She kept saying, "He's not like my ex. He doesn't do things like my ex. My ex was totally focused on me; he practically worshipped me when we were together." Well, the obvious answer to that is *there is a reason he's your ex*! In Julie's case, it was because he was moonlighting on the weekend with other women. Julie had finally decided enough was enough with her ex-hubby, but she went on her date with such high expectations, thinking, *This guy is really going to have to win me over and woo me.*

She put a block up with those expectations. It wasn't that he wasn't into her; he was just being himself, a guy who was the total opposite of Julie's ex: a guy who had a huge personality and liked to have fun, who thought he could make friends anywhere and at any time—and he usually did. By going on a second date, Julie was able to give him another chance as well as give herself the opportunity to let down her wall and let go of her ex. Now they're together, and it has been more than three months.

What happened to Julie on the first date is exactly what can happen to you if you go on your date with expectations. Those expectations will be a barrier between you and your ability to see the other person. You never know what you're going to find, so don't try to predict it. The only thing you can actually expect is for you to be yourself.

Lose the Labels

Julie labeled her date by saying "He's not like my ex." You don't want to label anybody, but especially on a first date. There should be no "this guy reminds me of so and so" or "this girl reminds me of the last girl I was with." By doing that, you're projecting bad energy and you aren't seeing the person for who he or she really is.

A little while ago I set up a gorgeous blonde woman with a really handsome guy. She thought he was great, but she told me that he totally screwed himself up by wearing a horrible 1960s cowboy shirt. He, in turn, was very nervous, his hands were sweating, and he was thinking, "Oh, my gosh. I don't know if I can handle a girl this beautiful." As soon as they both did that, they projected bad energy and shut each other down—she negatively judged his style, and he negatively judged what he was capable of. I told her to go on a second date, I gave him some wardrobe advice, and they got to date three. They're still friends.

Don't let the situation take control of you; you have to take control of it. Labeling someone and projecting bad energy isn't taking control. Keeping yourself focused on the person in front of you, and not on whomever you're reminded of, lets you be in complete control of reality rather than having a conversation with yourself in your own head. When you do the latter, you start to make assumptions about people rather than acknowledging them for who they are. When you notice yourself putting a label on someone else, just say to yourself, *I'm not going to start assuming these things. I don't have any evidence of what's going on except the person in front of me. Let me pay attention to this person now.*

Choose a Neutral Location

A date is stressful, exciting, and nerve-wracking. You want to make it as comfortable as possible for yourself and for your date so that the two of you can really focus on connecting your energy. Meet someone in an easy, low-key setting, like a coffee shop or a quiet restaurant. It doesn't have to be a serious, intimate setting, either. Go bowling or to the zoo! It'll be like you're a kid again, and you'll be more comfortable behaving as you naturally and normally would.

I strongly encourage that you do something in nature. If you can meet outside, that's great. When you're outside there's an abundance of energy and space. When you're in a confined space (whether it's crowded, loud, or small), it's easier for your energy to feel confined, and you'll automatically feel more nervous than you already were.

I also strongly discourage you from going somewhere exceedingly expensive. This is a common first-date mistake: "I'm going to take my date to the fanciest, most expensive restaurant I can think of because I want to impress her." First, aren't *you* enough to impress your date? Second, don't you think that a *lasting* relationship would more likely be based on someone being impressed by how much you make him or her laugh? Or how much you know about your common interests?

I tell 90 percent of my clients to meet for coffee and doughnuts for the first date. If they aren't into coffee, I suggest ice cream. Both coffee shops and ice cream shops are low-key environments, which means you get to really focus on the person you're with. Also, most people can afford either coffee or ice cream, so you don't have to worry about the cost. And what if the date goes completely sour? Do you really want to be out a $100 lobster dinner? Most people like coffee or ice cream or both.

Furthermore, you can enjoy both of these things for as little as thirty minutes or up to a few hours, depending on how the conversation is going. If you're really into it, order a second cappuccino. If you're really not, be done once you finish your sundae. There's no reason to sit through a three-course dinner with someone you don't find yourself connecting to. At least the nervous and jittery first date will be done with. and you can move on to the second date with a better idea of the person you're going out with. Finally, if worse comes to worst, if he ain't sweet, at least the ice cream will be!

Always Go Out Alone

I know that it is sometimes tempting to bring friends along, especially if you're nervous—but don't. You want your focus to be on the other person only, and if your friends are there, your attention and your energy will be divided. If you've gone the online dating route and are going on a date with someone you haven't met before, it's definitely safer to go to a location where other people will be around, but that doesn't mean you should bring your friends.

One of my clients took his date to a pottery class, and they had a blast! They were feeling so connected and having so much fun that he invited her to come along with him to a birthday party he'd been invited to that night. His ex happened to be at the birthday party, and so his date met his ex. His ex proceeded to air his dirty laundry: "Let me save you some time and trouble," bashing him to his date. As a result, they didn't keep dating.

This is just one example of what can happen. Granted, you may not always run into your ex while you're on a date with a new person just because you decide to go out with your friends. You never know what's going to be said about you, and you want to be sure that you have control in the situation. And most important, you don't want to be splitting the attention you're giving your date with anyone else.

Always Sit Across from Each Other

If you choose to go out to eat or for coffee, you should sit at a table or a booth with the other person across from you. If possible, try not to sit near other people. You want to be somewhere quiet where you can feel each other's rhythm and vibration. That is what you're looking for—to sense the other person's energy and determine whether it's an energy that pairs well with yours.

By positioning yourself across from each other, you'll be able to read the person you're on the date with better and get a truer sense of how you feel about him or her right from the start.

Just as you should avoid loud and crowded places because they're distracting, you should also avoid sitting side by side, because you will be distracted by what's in front of you. That's just human nature. So put the person you *want* to be paying attention to in front of you. You want to be able to look into each other's eyes. Always keep your eyes on your date; never lose eye contact. Don't stare each other down, but stay focused on each other. The eyes are the windows to the soul, and you want to always be connecting.

Absolutely No Texting

Do absolutely nothing that distracts you, but texting is the number one culprit in these situations. Even if there is a potential spark between you, nine times out of ten, if you're texting on the date, the other person will think you're losing interest in him or her. If your date is not right in front of you but is, for example, in the restroom, you can quickly check your phone if you need to. And by *need* I mean if you hired a babysitter for the evening and have to check in. Otherwise leave your phone in your purse or your pocket.

If you're texting, then talking, then texting, then talking, you will appear to have lost interest in the person you're with, who will in turn lose interest in you. If you leave your phone out on the table or if you're texting your friends while you're on a date, you're putting a wall between yourself and the person you're with. It's just one more barrier between you and the process of getting to know each other. You're not multitasking, you're multiswitching—moving back and forth between two things, giving each thing half your attention rather than giving one your full attention. If you're really looking to make a soul connection, you need to have your heart and your hands free to be able to do that, and you need to really focus in on the person who is in front of you, not the screen.

Say Thank You

Although you should definitely say thank you during the date for the kind things the other person does, it's also really important that you always thank your date at the end. Thank people for taking the time out of their schedule to meet with you, whether you expect to see them again or not. You never know what will happen. You never know when you're going to bump into them again. I always think it's better to do things with honey than vinegar.

At the end of the date, even if you think there's no way on God's green earth that you will ever see the person again, say, "Thank you for meeting me. It was nice to meet you. You seem like a really great person, I'm just not feeling a connection. I hope you find a person you connect well with, and if I meet someone I think would work for you, I'll keep your name and number in mind."

The rule of three should be adhered to as often as possible; that is, you should plan to go on at least three dates with the person. But you also need to be honest with yourself. If there's no way that you ever want to see this person again, you can go ahead and end it. But that doesn't mean you shouldn't be polite. You may be in the same place at a later time, and you always want to have positive energy flowing.

I had a client who went out with a guy, and it didn't turn out well. He was going through a divorce and really wasn't ready to date. He wasn't showing my client a lot of interest. So she ended the date, but with gratitude. Five years later they were at the same party. They ended up talking and then dating, and now they're together!

You don't always get to know what the universe has in store for you. But never say never; it might not work out today, but it could be great tomorrow.

Sometimes you're in the wrong place at the wrong time. The universe hasn't given you the time to get things together, or that might be the case for the other person. It could just be that whatever people are going through at that time is making them unable to focus their energy on you. You don't always get to know what the universe has in store for you. But never say never; it might not work out today, but it could be great tomorrow.

An Extra Reminder for the Gentlemen

I like to give this advice to men: Always take a rose when meeting your first date. This is something very sweet and simple that you can do to show your date that you appreciate her taking the time to be with you. Even if you never see her again, at least you're showing her that you're a nice guy. Florists usually sell a single rose, or you can quickly swing by the grocery store on your way. This small gesture may also help your date to open up to you a little more quickly emotionally, because from the very beginning you're showing her that you're thoughtful.

What to Do with These Reminders

Take your time with these reminders. I don't expect you to read this today, memorize it, and go out on your first date tomorrow. You have to remember that setting these rules is about you respecting yourself and the person you're going on the date with. So take some time to get comfortable with the reminders, and really commit to *all* of them in your heart.

Once you have done so, you're ready for your first date! And always remember, we're not here for a long time, we're here for a good time! Go have some fun!

Chapter 7

How to Keep the Energy Flowing

How did your first date go? If you're not completely certain, ask yourself the following key questions:

- Was I comfortable?
- Did dating this way feel different than it normally feels?
- What was different?
- Did I feel a spark between myself and the other person?
- Am I ready for a second date?

The last question should be fairly easy to answer. Unless the first date was completely atrocious and you were getting an awful vibe from the person, then you have to follow rule number one: always go on a second date. Let me explain why.

On the first date there can be physical energy but not a strong spiritual connection. That's totally normal, because on the first date you're not sharing yourself completely with the other person. Often people leave the first date thinking, *That person was great and seems wonderful, but I'm just not sure that I feel connected to him [or her]*. It's possible that your unconscious mind might be fearful of connecting with that person.

Before the first date you might not know what the person looks like, and you probably don't have any idea what you're walking into. By the second date, when you're more relaxed and open because all those jitters that come with the unknown are over and done with, the conversation can move more smoothly and you can focus on whether there really is something there for you. On the second date you're creating new space together. You never know what could happen when you open yourself up like that.

I had a client who got divorced about a year and a half ago. Since then she has done a lot of work and is in a great space in her life; she has really come out of her shell. She is so happy and alive because she has put so much energy into herself. She was extremely nervous about her first date: she was feeling sweaty and even told me that her ears were turning red. I told her to act as though she were merely going out with a good male friend.

On the first date she followed all the rules that I had set out for her (the ones discussed in Chapter 5); she and her date even maintained direct eye contact with each other. After the first date she was still nervous—she kept wondering if she had done the right things. She thought the guy was great, and she liked him, but she didn't feel physically attracted to him even though he had all the qualities she was looking for. I encouraged them to go on a second date.

She was a little reserved and didn't feel all that excited about the second date, but she went anyway. Even though before she thought that they didn't really have any chemistry, now she thinks there's potential. They've already agreed to have a third date.

This is incredibly common, especially when you first start dating (or start dating again). It's so easy to leave the first date and think, *I really don't know*. Nine times out of ten, that's just you, not the other person: you're putting up a wall because you're not entirely sure that you want to be in a relationship, or you're not feeling entirely confident in yourself. Well, if you don't know, go gather some more information. Go on the second date and learn more about the other person and yourself! You won't know by overanalyzing the same information. You have to get some new information before you commit to a decision.

Making Time for the Second Date

It doesn't matter how busy you are; the first three dates should occur within three weeks. Let's say your first date is on a Saturday night. I'd like you to see each other again by Wednesday night so that you don't lose interest in each other. If you're really flying high on the strong connection you feel, you can definitely see each other again in less than twenty-four hours. For instance, if you went out for dinner on Saturday night, you can definitely go out for brunch on Sunday morning. Trust your instincts: if they're telling you to give your time to this person, do it!

Just make sure that you're giving yourself enough time to really process what's going on and to truly consider what about the person attracts you. You also need to have time to recall the first date and the things you learned about this person: What are his hobbies? Do you remember what she told you about her dog? Do you remember how you felt sitting together?

You don't have to think about these things for a long time—remember, you don't want to overanalyze what's happening. How you feel in your gut is going to tell you more about what that person means to you than anything else. But you should have enough time to commit some things to memory so the person knows that you've been thinking about him or her in the meantime.

If someone has an extremely hectic schedule and has been up front with you about that, you need to ask yourself whether you think he or she is worth the wait. If you do think so, go out on the weekends—three weekends in a row. Don't let the three dates span longer than three weeks. You'll fall out of sync with each other's energy and let other things get in the way of the relationship.

You also need to be sure that this individual is prioritizing dating in the same way that you are. If you've cleared out as much of your schedule as you can to ensure that three dates can happen within three weeks, but the other individual can't see you for a second date for another month, it may be a good idea to nip this in the bud. People who do this either aren't in the same place as you when it comes to dating, or their lives don't currently lend themselves to thinking about dating the way you do.

Don't Be Afraid to Call

If you haven't heard from the other person after the first date, don't be afraid to pick up the phone and call. He or she may be interested in you but feel a little intimidated or uncertain about moving forward, thinking that you're the one who's not interested. Sometimes you meet someone you have a great connection with but then never hear from him or her again. The phone works both ways, however, so pick it up and make the second date happen.

I had a client who went on a first date with a guy she thought was incredible. She liked him a lot, and it seemed to be mutual. He said he would love to see her again, but he never texted her back when she texted him after the date. So I told her to pick up the phone and give him a call. She took the lead and called him and told him she thought he was really interesting, and in the course of the conversation they set up the second date.

After their phone call she told me, "I think I'm going to have to be the driver in this relationship, at least for the first few months." I totally agreed. This happens all the time. We get lost in things that are about us, such as did we scare the other person off with something we said? Don't leave yourself hanging!

The Second Date

Once you're on the second date, let your guard down a little bit more than you did on the first date and just enjoy your time together. Take a deep breath, and if you're still feeling nervous, just reassure yourself, *I've got this!* Your goal on this date is to really focus on opening yourself up for a new energy current that you're trying to create with the other person. Every date should be fun! Don't act as though you're on a hunt for a partner. It won't work if you put that need out there so strongly. You have to just think, *I'm here. I'm having fun. I'm just going to experience this.* You also have to simply trust the other person.

Now let's look at some do's and don'ts for the second date.

Share What You Want in a Relationship

Sharing what you want in a relationship is fine on the second date, but not before that. The first date is for getting as much information as you can about the person; on the second date, it's okay to start opening yourself up more, such as by talking about what you're looking for in a relationship. You need to be confident about what that is before you can share it with someone else, however, so ask yourself the following questions:

- Am I looking for a serious relationship?
- Am I looking for friendship?
- Am I just playing the field and trying to figure things out?
- Am I looking for my soul mate?

If you answered yes to one of these questions, be sure that's *truly* what you're ready for—and you are the only one who can answer that. So spend some time thinking about it before committing to it. When you're sure, you'll be able to easily and confidently articulate that to yourself and to your date.

Letting other people know this helps them to understand what you're looking for and gives them the opportunity to share with you what they're looking for. It's entirely possible that the amazing woman you took out for the first time last week is looking for her soul mate while you're just trying to figure things out. This does not mean that you should try to speed yourself up in order to not lose her. Even though you're at different places in your life, you can still be friends, and you certainly can *always* be learning from whomever you're with.

This also works the other way. If you're looking for your soul mate, but the incredible guy you went out with two nights ago is just playing the field, this doesn't mean that you should slow down your process or go backward in your learning just to be with him. People come into our lives for a reason, and that reason isn't always to give us exactly what we want. As long as you're loving the one you're with (yourself!), it will be very easy to say, "I'm feeling connected to you, but since we're at different places in what we're looking for, maybe we could just be great friends!"

Never Talk About Your Horrible Ex

Please don't talk about your ex-husband or your past girl-friend. You don't want to put bad vibes out there. You don't want your dates wondering whether they're going to become that in your mind.

My client Irvin is a tall, dark, handsome, and well-to-do man. He went out with a woman who was very smart and very together. However, she started talking about her ex-husband, who was a loser: he never paid child support. She thought that he was really selfish; during their marriage he was always work-ing and had neglected her as a result. They got a divorce, and there was a back-and-forth battle between them for a long time.

Irvin was really interested in the woman originally. He thought their chemistry and energy was great. But then she bashed her ex-husband into the ground. He said it was so bad that the only thing that was missing was the nail in the heart. He decided that this was not going in the right direction at all. He told me, "I did not sign up for this. She was so smart and together, but when she bashed this guy, I just kept thinking, *I don't want to be that guy!* She still has a lot of anger and hostility, and she didn't seem to be moving forward." He concluded that he didn't want to even be in the category of dating her—he was sure she would be putting that negative energy into him because she was still so wrapped up in her ex.

Irvin was completely right. You definitely should not talk about your ex on your second date. The person you're dating does not want to walk into fire, and that's what such a situation is going to feel like.

Never Talk About Your Amazing Ex

Sometimes the opposite happens. Sometimes you're still hung up on your ex, who was awesome. Maybe you believe you split up prematurely, or your ex left for reasons you can't understand yet. Even though you might think that's a positive conversation to have with your new date, it isn't—at least, not on the second date.

Let me tell you what happened with John, Judith, and Kim. Judith is one of my clients. She went on a date with John and was totally into him. They were interacting really smoothly, and the chemistry was great. Then John started talking about his ex, Kim, and how much he loved her and what a great relationship they had had. Kim and John were together for more than seven years, but Kim was so crazy in love with John that she became really jealous and obsessive. If he even just talked to another woman, she would freak out at him.

Ever since John and Kim split up, he hasn't been able to go out with someone else and connect with her. But now he was beginning to connect with Judith. John's connection to Kim made Judith hesitant, however. How do you get through to a guy who is still in love with his ex and can't get her out of his mind, even though his ex is now remarried?

The fact is that John will probably always love Kim. Even though he's open to a new relationship, because he has a standard based on Kim in his mind, he will have a hard time finding the right fit. John's future partner will have to have a great deal of patience and faith; she will have to be willing to stick by him as he works through the layers of his relationship with Kim and learn how to coach him through the process.

Judith actually chose to stay with John, and they've been in a relationship for a year now, but at first she wasn't entirely sure that she wanted to make that kind of commitment to a man who was still into someone else. This can easily happen in the early stages of dating, when you're still trying to figure yourself out.

If you're not sure whether to say something on your second date, ask yourself the following questions:

- If the person I'm on a date with said this to me, would I feel uncomfortable?
- Am I really close enough to this person to share such a deep part of me?
- If I start to talk about my ex, will I be able to stop?

Whether you carry hurtful feelings or positive feelings with you from a past relationship, getting on a topic that you can't get off means that you'll monopolize the conversation rather than having a dialogue. If someone wants to know about your past relationships, keep your answer to one sentence, such as "I dated someone for two years, but things didn't work out," and move on until later.

Avoid Words Like Hate and Never

If your date really likes to go bowling, don't say, "I hate bowling." If someone says, "I really want to go skydiving," don't reply, "I would never do that." First, that shuts down the conversation rather than encouraging the other person to continue sharing things. Second, you never know how important that activity might be to that person, and saying something negative may be offensive. Finally, by responding like that about new experiences, you are setting a limit on yourself when realistically you don't know what could happen tomorrow or how much you might enjoy trying something different.

I had a client who went on a date with a man who said he would never go to Europe because he hated traveling. She absolutely refused to go on a third date with him because she wanted to travel and see new places. She figured that this man's unwillingness to travel would mean that she would not have the kind of companion she was hoping to have in those adventures, so she automatically chose to eliminate him as a potential partner.

The only real *never* is that you never know what can happen or what you might be willing to do. Love is blind. You might move to Africa if you really love someone. If you have a great relationship, it doesn't matter where you live; the two of you will be able to create a nice space anywhere. When you're in a closely connected relationship, the sky is the limit.

Similarly, you should add to the rule from the first date about never labeling a person: don't label the relationship. Don't say, "Oh, this guy lives in Nebraska, and I would never move there. Who wants to live in Nebraska?" Plenty of people want to live in Nebraska, and you might want to, too, if you have a strong enough connection to someone there.

> **Being in a relationship means learning to be flexible and compromise.**

Being in a relationship means learning to be flexible and compromise. You have to learn new and different things, and you are getting an incredible opportunity to expand your sense of self. Just as you would probably get bored with a partner who likes all the same things that you like, being with a partner who constantly agrees with you about every plan you have for your life limits the amount that you get to learn in the relationship. You have to be willing to take up something the other person likes because that is an important part of learning about the person. I don't like to golf, but I took up golf to have a sport to play with my husband. You just have to throw yourself out there; being with that person may make whatever it is much more enjoyable.

Set Up the Third Date

By the end of the second date you should be ready to set up where you want to go on the third date, because you have learned so much about the person. By doing this, you're letting your date know that you're interested and willing to try things that he or she likes, not just the things that you like. It's very helpful for the third-date activity to be something that keeps you moving. By moving around with the other person, you'll let your energy flow more freely. But if you prefer to make plans to do something that doesn't involve much movement, that's okay.

For instance, if your date really likes bicycling, you can say, "Why don't we do something fun together next time that you like doing? Why don't we ride bikes?" This lets your date know that you remembered at least one thing about him or her. I suggest that you frequently address your date by name, but in particular when setting up the third date. It indicates not only that you know who he or she is but also that you're serious.

Always End with (Only) a Kiss

At the end of the second date, you should kiss—but *just* a kiss, not more than that. It doesn't have to be a deep or prolonged kiss, just a kiss on the lips. This is one way to know whether you have a connection with the person. If someone is not a "good kisser," in your opinion, what that really means is that you're not feeling a connection.

By kissing your date, you're letting him or her know that you're open to going out on a third date. You'll be thinking about each other after the date and will go to sleep happy. Kissing on the second date also makes you excited to see each other on the third date because perhaps you'll get to do that again.

Yet just because you've kissed after the second date, this doesn't mean that you should let yourself get carried away. Don't go to either of your homes together at the end of the date. You never know what could happen once the two of you are alone in a space with a bed. You might end up doing something that it's too soon to be doing. You might screw yourself up for your third date.

Stop Analyzing!

When you start to analyze the relationship or the other person, you're putting a wall up; you're protecting yourself from being loved. Don't spend much time trying to analyze the connection, because you can talk yourself out of something that could be really good. This usually has a lot to do with your own past experiences. If you find yourself doing a lot of analyzing, you may need to stop and ask yourself whether you're really ready for love. You might not find it because you're not ready for it. That's something only you can answer. And you must be honest with your answer.

> **If you find yourself doing a lot of analyzing, you may need to stop and ask yourself whether you're really ready for love.**

If you're one of those people who keeps analyzing every little piece of the relationship or the other person's actions, remind yourself that you're not perfect. No one is. If the other person analyzed everything you said or did during the course of the dates, how would you stand up? Probably not too hot. Give him or her a break, and give yourself a break. Instead of analyzing, trust your gut. You've opened yourself up and done work on your third chakra (your gut), so go ahead and trust it.

The Third Date

Have you ever had this experience before? You go to a restaurant for the first time, and it's amazing. The service is great, and the food arrives hot and tastes delicious. Your glass is refilled before it ever has a chance to get empty, and you're so pleased that you commit to going again. But on the second visit, the server doesn't take your drink order right away and then forgets the extra side of guacamole you asked for, and you have to get someone's attention in order to get some more iced tea. You think, *What the heck? I'm never going back there again, because it was awful!*

This has happened to almost everyone I've ever talked to. You could look at it two ways: the time you went and got great service was a fluke, or the time you went and things were horrible was a fluke. You just don't know which is which until you try again.

The same is true with people. On a first date you might be uncomfortable, and they might seem awkward. Maybe they're just nervous. On the second date they might seem like they're rushing to get things over with; maybe they are—some people are *always* in a rush, or maybe they have extra work to finish up once they get home. You just won't know until you try again.

This is why you have to go on at least three dates before you decide to move on. If after three dates this person is still nervously awkward or is still in a rush, move along, if that's not your thing. Just like baseball, dating can be a "three strikes you're out" scenario.

But let's say you somehow end up at that restaurant for a third time despite trying to avoid it. If the service is as great as, or even better than, the first time you went, what will you think? Maybe the server you had the second time was the only one in the restaurant, was preoccupied with a sick child, or had final exams to contend with. The third time indicates which way the situation is likely to go in the future.

The same thing is true with people: you don't just have to give them a chance, you have to give them more than one chance. Some people take longer to get comfortable than others, and some people might take longer to get comfortable with *you* than others. Everyone is different. But if you allow yourself to give someone else a chance, you never know what you'll find.

Going on three dates, even if they don't work out, isn't wasting your time. You should be going on every date with the intention to learn and have fun. There's nothing wasteful about learning, and there's definitely nothing wasteful about having fun. Remember, we're not here for a long time, we're here for a good time!

Now let's look at some do's and don'ts for the third date.

Sit Next to Each Other, Not Across from Each Other

Whether you're on a date that involves a lot of sitting or a lot of moving, now you should sit side by side as often as you can.

Doing this will help you determine whether there is any physical connection. Sitting next to each other will help your energies connect more closely.

See Your Future in Their Eyes

As I said earlier, you should maintain eye contact with each other throughout your first and second dates. On the third date, I want you to look into each other's eyes and see if you can see yourself through their eyes. Can you see yourself with that person ten years down the road? If the answer is yes, then you absolutely want to take the time to get to know this person further. If the answer is no, it's time to move on.

You could look at the person's entire body and say, "I could be with this woman because she's a good height for me" or "I could be with this man because he has large muscles." By looking in the person's eyes, however, you'll be able to discern whether this is a strong enough soul connection to keep you together regardless of what the rest of the person's body is like.

Figuring Out the Connection

Take dating one step at a time. Life is a gamble—in relationships, as in everything we go through in life, we might win and we might lose. Either way, you have to feel confident enough about yourself that you're going to learn from these dates. Even if you don't see the person again, you will have learned something that will make you feel much more confident the next time. It's like fishing: you get a fish on the line and do the work to reel it in. Then you have to decide whether it's big enough or good enough or the right kind. If it's not, you throw it back in the water and don't have it for dinner.

There are a number of ways that figuring out the connection between you could go: you might be into the other person or might not; the other person might be into you or might not. Where you are might not match up with where the other person is. So let's look at the ways this could go.

You Don't Feel a Connection but the Other Person Does

After three dates, if you're just totally not into the other person, the best way to end it is fast. The longer you let it linger, the longer the other person will hold on to the hope of winning you over. If you're not feeling a connection by the end of the third date, it's not going to happen in the future.

Yet even if there are no sparks and looking into your date's eyes reveals nothing to you, you still should be nice to the person, because karmic payback is a bitch. You don't want to be rude, because it will come back to you. You should say, "It was really nice meeting you. I think you're a great person—a wonderful person, even—but I'm just not feeling a connection. I need to be with someone I feel connected to. I want you to have that kind of connection, too. I'll definitely keep your name and number in mind if I meet someone I think would be great for you." It's the same thing you'd say on the first date if you were sure by then that you really weren't into the person. Just end it.

It's much more polite to just move on. Keep in mind that you want the other person to find a connection, too. If you let the dates you're rejecting know that you're interested in them getting to be in the kind of relationships that they want, it will make the situation easier. You want to let them down gently, not with anger or aggression.

You do have to be firm about it, however, so you don't have to worry about them calling or texting or wondering where you are. If they really press you and say, "Oh no, we just need to give it a little more time," think that through. Do you really not feel it? Or are you just blocking yourself? If you're certain that you really don't feel it, say, "I'm really in tune with myself, and I can already tell that there's not a connection." End it. Don't let it linger. That way the other person gets to move on, and so do you. Try to end it on a good note even if the person gets upset or angry. Two wrongs don't make a right. Remember, it's always best to do things with honey and not vinegar.

Never feel obligated. Don't think that you have to go out with the person again. You don't. Being direct and getting straight to the point is much kinder to the person than pretending you want to be with someone when you don't. Think about how you would feel if someone did that to you. Be truthful: you know it would not feel good. If you're not able to connect with the person and you try to give it more time, you could miss out on Mr. or Ms. Right. Always remember, we're not here for a long time, we're here for a good time!

Don't say, "You were really great. I'm super busy these next few days, but I'll try to fit you in." Just be honest. If you don't think there's a future with each other, say so; don't lead anyone on. As guilty as you may feel expressing your honest opinion, it's for the best. You've given it three dates. You've already put time and energy into this person. If it's not working, you're not obligated to *make* it work; you both just need to move on.

You Feel a Connection but the Other Person Doesn't

Do you see yourself with this person twenty years down the road? You have to put that image in your mind, heart, and soul. Do you feel open enough to recognize whether there is a connection on both sides? Go ahead and ask whether the other person actually feels a connection. You should be able to say, "Hey, I feel like there's a connection. You have great energy. You have a great smile." Find something that you like about the person and mention it as you're saying that there's a connection.

If other people are not feeling what you are feeling, ask your-self whether you want to give it more time and space. If you do, tell them you're feeling a connection, that you'll give them some space and time, and that you'd be happy to be their friend. Something might happen in the future; you never know. Some-times being friends leads to something more. But you have to ask yourself how much time and energy you want to put into it.

This happens all the time: You really feel the connection between yourself and other people. You really like them and think that they're into you. But when you let them know that you feel connected, they tell you they just don't. I always ask my clients, How much effort are you willing to put into this relationship? Anything worth working on is worth waiting for. If you really believe this is the strongest connection you've ever had, this could be your soul mate. You don't want to be pushy with the person, though, and you don't want to be demanding.

Maybe these people are feeling something for you that they haven't felt in a long time, and maybe they're just scared. It's not always about you. Sometimes it's just that they've been hurt in the past. It might not be that they're not into you—they might just not be ready for you. You might be more than they can handle.

To figure out which it is, you have to trust your gut instincts. You can't go with your heart or your mind. Ask questions like "When we're together, do you feel chemistry?" If the person says yes, it might be worth it to give him or her space and time. If the person says no, just acknowledge that you have felt this way about someone else. Accept it, cut the cord, and cut your losses. Thank these people for their time and be done.

Don't get discouraged. This relationship, these three dates, may be preparing you for something bigger and stronger—something so great it can't even really be explained in words. Always keep your head above water, whether the three dates were amazing or horrible. Don't let energy vampires suck the life out of you. They can't do that unless you let them.

Of course it's going to be hard. You just have to remember that everything in life is a lesson. It could be part of your karma—maybe you needed to learn this lesson. Even if it was a negative experience, it could end up being a great one if you let yourself learn from it. Remember, there are no problems, only solutions.

If you've met someone and feel an awesome connection, so that now you're finding that it's hard to get over him or her, know that there's no secret potion to make this person want you. Even if you could do something to *make* someone want you, it probably wouldn't work out because you're not being honest about who you are.

Take time to meditate. This will help you focus on yourself more. You have to figure out how to let go of the person's energy. Make a list of the things you want. Take the things from that relationship and that person—all the things you wanted that you had in that relationship—and write them down.

Take what you've written down and make a vision board—that is, post the list on a bulletin board or a wall. Maybe that person has a lot of qualities that you want in someone but lacks others. Perhaps you'll find a lot of those characteristics in the next person you're with. By being clear on what those qualities are, you'll be able to use that energy to attract a new person.

Even when someone isn't the right person for you, you're still going to find Mr. or Ms. Right, because being with that person has opened you up to being with the right person. By creating the vision board, you'll be able to ask yourself, *What did I learn from this experience?* Maybe you discovered that what you thought you wanted was something different from what you really want. Maybe you learned how to say no. If you really meditate on it long and hard enough and ask God what your lesson was, God will lead you and show you the way.

And who knows, it could very well be that the person you were into was actually a butthead. You don't have any time for that.

Both of You Feel a Connection

Be verbal. Let the other person know you're really enjoying his or her company. There's no sense in not saying what you feel. Say that you want to keep the relationship moving. Use your voice! Don't be afraid to open up and express how much you're enjoying the person's company and how strong a connection you feel.

It's also important at this point to let the person know that you want to take it slow. Believe it or not, this makes people feel more comfortable because then they know that you're not in a rush—you want a quality relationship. You're not looking for the slam-bam-thank-you-ma'am kind of thing. Sometimes the other person isn't ready for the kind of commitment you might be ready for.

By saying that you want to take it slow, you're indicating that you're interested in the other person. It's not about *your* wants and needs, it's about his or hers, and you're interested in treading lightly and being certain. Keeping the relationship alive is about keeping your energy alive. Taking it slow, and *communicating* that you want

> **Keeping the relationship alive is about keeping your energy alive.**

to take it slow, gives you time and space to ensure that you'll continue feeling good and strong. When you have that kind of confidence, people feel it from you—it's a different kind of energy from anything else. Your dates will feel more confident voicing their own desires because of your confidence.

Wait Before You Try Again

If the three dates just didn't work out, for whatever reason, you should wait two or three weeks before you go out on another date. You absolutely should not go out on a date the next day. You need a break to clear out the energy from the last person in order to create space for the new person.

Write down all the things you didn't like about the last person you went out with. Write down the ways you didn't feel connected. Release the person's energy by writing his or her full name down on a sheet of paper (as many times as you want). Cut or rip it up into as many pieces as you like and flush it down the toilet. I'm completely serious—right down the toilet.

This is not an expression of anger or rage. It's just about letting go and getting that energy out of your space so that you can get ready for a new person's energy. Keeping the old energy is a way of procrastinating—you're holding yourself back by doing that. You didn't find Mr. or Ms. Right, but if you don't let go of that person's energy, you *still* won't be able to find Mr. or Ms. Right because you've held on to the bad energy inside you. You have to clear out the old and the worn-out to create space for a new relationship; you need to reconnect to yourself.

Take some time to do some of the meditation that we talked about in Chapter 2. Get engaged with nature and spend some time alone. Focus on doing something that makes you happy and helps you create new space.

Chapter 8

The Signs
of an Energy
Vampire

We've talked about the various responses you can have to the different kinds of connections you may feel. Anyone can have a connection with anyone, but that doesn't mean it will always be a positive influence in your life to be with a particular person. You need to trust your gut as you are dating; that's going to help you know whether you even have a connection, much more so than what the person looks like in the mirror or on paper. But you've also got to use your head a little bit, because there is something out there that I call the energy vampire, which can totally screw things up for you.

When your friends talk about dating, maybe you've heard them say things like "I should have seen that from the beginning" or "She was always like that, I just didn't think it was a big deal." Those things they "should have seen" are red flags. There are certain people who will suck out your energy by being negative or creating chaos in your life, just as we saw with Michael and Camilla. No matter what you do or how emotionally ready you are, the match will not work because this person's energy is toxic. Here are some characteristics of energy vampires to help you recognize one when you meet one.

They Only Talk About What They Own

I told you that on date number one you should keep your focus on the other person. You should encourage your dates to talk about themselves and what they like and don't like. But when people talk continually about the things they have, all the things they own, that means they think they're all big deals— and they're usually not.

When people try to woo you too much early on, if on the first three dates they're saying things like "I have a beautiful condo in Malibu I want to take you to," "I want to take you around the world," or "I want to give you my heart and soul," nine times out of ten these people are a crock. If those statements start coming up *later* in the relationship, once you've really gotten to know each other, that's really nice; it may mean that person is coming to understand what kinds of things you like. (If you love the beach and someone wants to take you on a beach vacation, that's awesome!) But if your date is a total Casanova right off the bat, run, don't walk! That person has a big head, too big to see you for who you really are.

They Won't Compromise

Let's say you're on the first or second date with a man. You say to him, "I'd love to go skydiving. It sounds so fun!" He says, "No way." So you say, "I see how skydiving could freak some people out. Would you want to go paddleboarding sometime?" Again he says, "No way." So you try a third idea: "I love to go to the beach. Would you like to go sometime?" He says, "No way." You could come up with a hundred more suggestions of things you like to do, and he would probably say, "No way" to most of them.

It's one strike, two strikes, three strikes—you're out! If people say no to three things, that's definitely a red flag. It means they won't compromise; they have no interest in making it easy for someone to *want* to be interested in them. Eventually you're going to get bored, annoyed, or pushed down. Someone who doesn't want to compromise doesn't care about what you want. Does that sound like being in a loving relationship? That person isn't ready to be in one. Walk away.

It's All About Them

Although the first date, as I've said, should be about getting to know the other person, this doesn't mean that everything should always be about him or her. Energy vampires want to be with you on *their* time, when *they* have the time available, not when it's also convenient for you. They want you to cancel your plans to fit into their schedule. Maybe they're even quick-tempered about it. When they're acting that way, they're not making an effort to be with you.

I had a client named Ron who was totally into a woman named Kelly. He wanted to marry her; he thought she was the one. Everything was going in the right direction, but the relationship eventually started to always be about what *he* wanted: where *he* wanted to go, what *he* wanted to do, what *he* wanted to eat. When they started to plan a vacation together, Ron wanted to go to Alaska to go mountain climbing. Kelly is terrified of heights, and climbing a mountain probably isn't the best way to get over that. Yet Ron's response was, "No, this is where we're going. These are the things we're going to do." It was never about her and where she wanted to go and what she wanted to do. He had to control the situation. The relationship finally died, and he lost a potential soul mate.

If you find yourself on a date with someone like Ron, I encourage you to respond the way that Kelly did. There's no sense in living a life that doesn't have the things you want in it. Although it's important to compromise with your partner, compromise never means only ever doing what he or she wants to do. If the road sign says the speed limit is forty-five miles per hour, don't go over fifty but don't go twenty-five, either. You need to find a balance.

Their Attention Wanders

If people can't look you directly in the eye, if they're talking away from you instead of toward you, if they are continually checking out the other men or women in the room, then they're not concentrating on you. Not making eye contact with you means that they're either hiding something or not confident in themselves, or possibly both. If their heads are clearly turned by the attractive individual across the room, that means they're only interested in a physical relationship with that person and with you. Red flag.

If they stumble over your name or don't even use it—if they start calling you "honey," "sweetie," or "baby"—walk away. They should remember your name and call you by it. And they shouldn't diminish it to a cute nickname; if you say your name is Susan and they keep calling you Susie, that tells you something. If they don't get your name right, they're probably just looking to get into your pants. What's the point in connecting with people like this when they can't even be bothered to know your name? Red flag. Move on.

They Disappear and Then Apologize

Let's say that you were supposed to go out with a woman on Friday night and she stood you up. You're able to let it go; you figure out how to move on from it and clear out the negative energy because you're becoming a pro at loving the one you're with. If she calls you three weeks later and tells you a big sob story—"I'm so sorry! I miss you. I want to be with you. Please give me a second chance!"—don't fall for it. If something had come up that night, even something tragic, if she cared about being with you, she would have let you know and canceled the date. Nine times out of ten people like that are playing the field; they connect with someone else, and when things don't work out with that person, they come back to you.

This is something you want to nip in the bud, because if you don't, disaster is looming. This is a double red flag.

I have a client I'll call Jenny who has been trying to date a certain guy for about six months. (He's not someone I matched her with.) She's having a hard time because he calls her and tells her, "I love you and care about you." After he says that, however, he goes incognito for three to six weeks. She says that when they're together the energy is great, but he tells her that he doesn't think he's good enough for her and that she deserves better. Then he disappears. Then he comes back and says the same thing again: "I love you, I care about you. I have to work on myself. I'm trying to find myself."

If you're truly going through something difficult, you should be able to identify with the other person and say, "I'm having a hard time right now; I just need a little bit of space." Jenny doesn't hear that from this guy; she calls and texts and gets nothing back from him until a few weeks later. When people do that to you—when they disappear, then call you later and apologize because they needed to take a hiatus to clear their mind—that's a bad sign. That's a run-for-your-life moment.

I understand that you want to be patient, that you think it's so poetic and insightful that these people are trying to find themselves. Are you *that* stupid that you can't see through it? You really think these people want to be with you? If they wanted to be with you and had a connection to you, they wouldn't disappear on you. You need to have more credibility for yourself. Say to yourself, "You know what? I respect myself, and this isn't a relationship I want to be in."

It happens quite often that people we once knew pop back into our lives. They'll say, "I was out last night and saw a guy who looked like you" or "You were in my dream last night." Don't let yourself be fooled by that. You're just getting played. You're smarter than that and deserve better.

If you find yourself in this situation, you may need to ask yourself whether you really want to be in a relationship or you just want to be loved so badly that you would let someone take advantage of you. If the latter is true for you, reread this book and take your time working through it. If you don't sort this stuff out, you will keep making the same mistakes and feeling the same pain.

They're Always Low on Cash

I'm not one to say that money matters, so this may seem out of the blue. But there's a difference between lending someone five dollars that you're paid back the next time you see each other and lending someone five dollars every time you're together. It's not about the material status of the person who has the money to lend—who cares? It's about the respect that comes with paying someone back.

You want someone to respect you. You may also want someone to take you to dinner and give you gifts, or you may want to buy the dinner and give the gifts. As long as there's a balance, things are fine. Happiness is not about having the most expensive gift, it's about having someone in your life who respects you for who you are. If you find that you're regularly paying for someone who is always promising to pay you back but never does, that's not okay. You need to check yourself.

I have a client named Sandy. She met a guy on the Internet who lives in another state. They've been in a long-distance relationship for about a year, and she says she is really feeling the vibe with him—she thinks they have a great connection and that he's the right person. Now, I think that meeting people on the Internet and having long-distance relationships are both totally okay. But in a long-distance relationship, you really need to be seeing each other every four to six weeks.

In Sandy's case, they're talking on the phone a lot (not through text messages). He tells her that he loves her and wants to be with her and that he's trying to get his life together so he can move to where she lives. In twelve months, they've seen each other three times. All three times they've done what he likes to do and gone where he likes to go; never mind what she's interested in! In addition, Sandy keeps paying for him. She gives him money to help his family. She pays not only his cell phone bill but his *siblings'* cell phone bills as well!

She thinks that by being with this guy she's going to give him what he needs. But Sandy is really insecure in herself. She wants to be loved so badly that she thinks that if she doesn't give this guy what he wants and do all the things he wants, she'll lose him. She keeps giving him money so he'll stay with her. It makes you wonder: What's he really with her for? For who she is or for the money she has?

Men and women can both be insecure; they can think that if they don't give their partners exactly what they need, they will lose them. If you're so scared of losing the person you're with, then this is not someone who is worth your time. I know that sounds like a contradiction. You need to take a good hard look at yourself. You need to come to a place inside yourself where you can feel whole, be loved, and laugh all on your own.

It always comes back to loving the one you're with. If you always give and give and give and don't receive, how does that make you feel? Kind of drained, right? That's no way to live, and that's a relationship you need to get out of in a hurry.

They Can't Take Criticism

There's certainly no reason to tell people on your first three dates to completely change their lives in order to be with you. But let's say that they've had a few too many drinks. You tell them, "You've had a little bit too much to drink. It might not be a good idea to drive home. How about I call you a cab?" But their reaction is "Oh, no. I'm fine. I can drive." Rather than taking it as a compliment that you were concerned about their safety, they continue to press the issue that they're fine. This shows that they can't take criticism. They also can't listen. That's a huge red flag.

This is something that happens a lot; I see it all the time. Clients say, "I want to be with this person, but he drinks a little too much, and when I say something he lashes out at me for it." He is basically saying, "I don't want to change. I am who I am." Someone who loves people like this isn't going to be able to change them. If people want to

If people want to change, they have to do it for themselves.

change, they have to do it for themselves. And if they make the change merely to please someone else, it won't be a real change because it isn't about them. But if they aren't willing to listen to people even about simple things, how will they ever come to make changes for themselves?

They Want You to Change

Let's say you get to the end of the third date and your date says, "You know what, I'm super into you. I feel really connected to you. I'm really just not attracted to you. If you were twenty pounds thinner [or heavier], I would be." Be who you are and love yourself, because that's the way God made you. Walk away from that double red flag. You can make that change for yourself if you want to, but not because someone else tells you that you should. It doesn't matter what size you are. Be you.

One topic that seems to come up all the time in my work with clients is religion. This can emerge as a point of contention on the first date or after a couple has been together for a year. Let me make it simple for you: people should not change their religion and be something that they're not unless they really want to. If someone even suggests it, that's a double red flag.

If the person you're with tells you that you have to belong to a certain faith in order for the two of you to be together, you have to ask yourself, *Am I feeling the connection with the religion? Or am I just feeling the connection with this person?* If it's the first, all power to you. If it's the second, don't do it. You change religions because you *want* to change religions.

This is very important: we are all God's children. God created humanity and *humanity* created religion. There is only one God, so if you believe in God and you believe in yourself and you put your faith in that, it doesn't matter what your religion is. Keep what you believe and respect the other person. If people tell you to convert to be with them, tell them you respect them and their faith, but you're sticking with what you believe. There's no reason, with enough respect, that two religions can't coexist in the same household. If someone still wants you to change your religion, walk away.

They're Jealous

Jealousy can come up in a number of different situations. Sometimes it's understandable. If you're on a date and you make out with someone else and your date gets jealous, that's totally understandable. This may sound like an extreme example, but what I'm trying to illustrate is that if you're physically acting on an attraction to someone else, it makes sense that the one you're dating becomes jealous.

But let's say you're on a date and your date mentions a celebrity or an actor who you think is smoking hot, and you voice that. If your date get offended and becomes jealous of that, that's a red flag. What are your odds in this world that you'll meet that celebrity or actor and have an affair? Probably pretty slim. It's normal for people to fantasize about someone they've never met. We all daydream to some extent. But if your date is so far out of touch with reality that this feels threatening, walk away. That person will probably shift from being jealous to being possessive.

In addition to protecting yourself from a possessive relationship, it's important to be aware that people feel jealous because they aren't secure in themselves. Nine times out of ten, if they're jealous like that, it's because they didn't grow up in a stable environment. Perhaps that's the way they saw their parents behave, and they haven't undone the negative things they learned as a child.

It's also not your responsibility to help them learn to do that. Actually, if you say, "I feel a really strong connection to you, but your jealousy isn't going to work for me," that may be just the thing that *does* help them.

They Stalk

Believe it or not, the worst thing in a relationship is overcommunication. People make a fuss about a lack of communication (which certainly isn't a great thing), but overcommunication can be worse. Let's say someone is calling you three or four times a day and you're replying that you don't think there's a lot of chemistry between you, but the person won't give up. That's not a healthy thing. You should completely stop responding to them.

I had a client named Tony who went out on a few dates with a woman named Blair. Tony really liked her; he felt a connection with her and thought she was good, sweet, beautiful, and intelligent. He began to let down his wall with her.

But then Blair became obsessed with him and got jealous. She constantly called and texted. She would show up at his house during the day while he was sleeping (he worked the night shift), and when he didn't answer the door, she concluded that he must have someone else. So she would sit outside his house in her car and watch for him to come out. Eventually he saw her one day when he took out the trash. He called her and asked her why she was in his neighbor's yard. She replied, "I was checking to see if you're home." He said, "Obviously I am. You're watching me take out my garbage." Tony had really been into her, so if she had taken a chill pill, maybe things would've worked out and he wouldn't have had to take out a restraining order on her.

If you're in the early stages of a relationship and you don't feel enough space to be yourself, or the person doesn't seem to trust you when you say where you are, don't walk away, run as fast as you can. Something as simple as a bunch of phone calls can quickly turn into a very serious and dangerous situation. Your gut will tell you when it's too much or if something about it doesn't feel right. Always trust your gut.

If you find yourself in a situation like Tony's, seek help from the police immediately. They will be able to provide you with information and resources to keep you safe.

* * *

If you find yourself in a relationship with an energy vampire, be quick about getting him or her out of your life, but understand that this person came into your life to teach you something. You should not, under any circumstances, keep people like this in your life while you try to figure that lesson out. Let them go and *then* learn.

Remember, you can have a soul connection with anyone. That connection is happening for reasons outside your control. But that soul connection does not, under any circumstances, mean that you should allow yourself to be used or harmed.

Chapter 9

When to Say Good-bye to Someone and Hello to Yourself Again

I have a client named Virginia who has been in a relationship with a man named Andy for a very long time. Andy has tried everything to make Virginia happy, to the point of doing the things that she likes in an attempt to adapt himself and make sure they have similar interests. But when Virginia sees him and is around him, her energy feels really low. When she's not with him, she feels great! She doesn't want to go home and be with him; in fact, she goes out specifically to be away from him.

Virginia feels bad about hurting her partner because he's trying so hard: he's doing everything in his power to change to be with her. But she just isn't opening herself up anymore, because she's ready to say good-bye. She knows that being with Andy will make him happy, but she feels like a shriveled-up prune because of the toxification in her body. She is starting to look not so good and feel not so good. She can feel Andy sucking the energy out of her.

When to Say Good-bye

How do you know when it's time to cut the cord, while your head is still attached to your body? Here are some warning signs.

You Want to Be Away

These are some of the things you may notice: You go out more without your partner, specifically because you want to be away from him or her. Or you close yourself in the bedroom frequently just to get away. Is that how things always were? If that's new to your relationship, take a look. Are you trying to get away from the person you're in a relationship with? You have to really ask yourself that. If the answer is yes, you have to look at why.

When the energy between you and your partner isn't flowing anymore, it could be for a number of reasons. It doesn't mean that the person is terrible to you or mean to you; in fact, it's often the opposite. Your energies just don't match up. Your partner thinks that you need to be together, and you don't. That's a toxic relationship. That's when you have to see the signs and get yourself out of that relationship. It doesn't matter how badly you want each other.

You Feel Sick a Lot

You may want to be away from your partner more often because when you're together you feel slow and a lack of energy. That's because your partner is sucking the energy out of you. It doesn't seem to matter how many sweet things he or she does, your energy is still low. In addition to feeling much slower, you may have also noticed that you're getting headaches when you're together or that your stomach is frequently upset.

If the doctor has no answer for your physical symptoms, it's probably that your partner is depleting your energy. It's probably not being done consciously, either. People don't usually do that intentionally. All that it means is that the two of you are not a good match. You have to get out of that relationship. It doesn't matter what your partner says or does, it's not going to work.

You Can't Stand the Person Touching You

Whenever your partner comes around, do you feel annoyed by it? Do you find your partner's voice annoying or touch repulsive? That means it's time to move on. You just don't feel the connection with this person anymore in any way, shape, or form. You have to let go.

You're Standing Still

Sometimes the relationship is not working anymore because that person isn't helping you move forward. Remember Camilla? She always had to pick up the slack from Michael— financially, around the house, and emotionally. She even moved to a new state to be with him (or because he wanted her away from him), so she didn't really have a chance to develop herself. Even though she was always moving, she wasn't really moving *forward*. Now think about Danielle and Andrew: Danielle talked about the balance that they found together and how they were both always learning from each other, even if the other one wasn't trying to teach. That's called emotional and spiritual movement. That's what you *want* in a relationship.

I had a client named Kyle. He went with a guy for all the wrong reasons: it was who his parents thought was right for him. He thought this relationship was what he needed because everyone was telling him it was—that they should get married and live happily ever after. But inside, they just couldn't seem to get to the next level of commitment with each other. Kyle had to walk away from that guy because he was being held back by the relationship. He was trying to make other people happy instead of himself, and as a result both he and his relationship lost momentum.

Sometimes your partner's negativity is what's blocking you. You may even find that you feel like you're moving but that the movement is backward instead of forward. That's when you have to cut the cord and move on, doing whatever it takes. A true psychic match will nurture you in such a way that you will always be moving forward because of the relationship.

A true psychic match will nurture you in such a way that you will always be moving forward because of the relationship.

How to Say Good-bye

When you find yourself in a situation like Virginia's, you have to tell yourself: *My partner has great energy, but the relationship is just not working.* This was simply a learning experience, part of what you were meant to go through in this life. You had to connect with that person for various reasons. All your dating experiences are about learning. Before you cut the cord, you have to ask yourself, *Do I see myself with this person ten years down the road? Is this the person God truly wants me to be with?* If you're not feeling good energy, then it's not the one God wants you to be with, and you're not the one God wants your partner to be with, either.

This relationship is just one part of what you came here to do energetically, mentally, physically, and spiritually. This relationship is about your identity being formed. You have to say

> You can't stop others from taking the journey they're meant to be on; that will only bring negative energy into your life.

good-bye to the person so both of you can move on to the next chapter in your lives. You can't stop others from taking the journey they're meant to be on; that will only bring negative energy into your life.

But how do you actually do it? How do you actually tell someone good-bye?

Use Words

The faster you get out of the relationship, the better it is for both of you. If you stay in it after you've already closed your heart to that person, the relationship starts to become mean. The other person starts to resent you. So use words. Tell the person point-blank, "I love you. I care about you. But I'm not *in* love with you. I don't feel the same way about you that you feel about me. Our energies are at different levels. If I'm no good for me, then I'm not good for you, either. If I am to grow and find my center and get what I need to be healthy, this isn't going to work. I'm not saying you're not a great person, I'm just saying that I'm not at the same place you are. As much as I care about you, it's not good for me or for you. The best thing for me to do is to find my way and my own space."

The other person needs to move on, too, and be able to find love and happiness. There are a lot of fish in the sea, and I hope you'll both have better luck next time. You'll each get to the right person someday. Sometimes you have to go through these experiences in order to better understand what kind of person you want to be with in the future. It's always better to do things with honey than with vinegar. Choosing to let someone go whom you're not 100 percent into is the kinder thing to do.

Cut It Off and Let Them Go

I know that it can be very hard to let someone go, even when you know that it's time to move on. Letting someone go is like losing a life; saying good-bye to someone and knowing that you're not going to see each other again is one of the hardest things to do. You'll feel bad. You'll want to call, e-mail, or text to make sure that the person is feeling okay.

Don't do it.

When you pick up the phone or send an e-mail or a text message, you're giving people false hope. They'll think that they still have a chance with you because you're still expressing care for them. And that's exactly right: you probably do still care for them, especially if this was a hard decision to make. This is why you need to let them go. The best way to do it is to cut off contact completely.

Don't keep up with them just because you feel guilt. Don't look back. You have to keep moving forward because if you don't, you'll be sitting by yourself on a rock for ninety years, and while you're on that rock, no one will want to be with you. So let old lovers go, because your time with them is over.

Cutting them off and letting them go are actually different things that go together. Cutting them off means not communicating with them anymore. Letting them go means mentally and spiritually clearing them from you. The reality is they will move on. They might never really like you again. That doesn't always feel great to think about. But you have to let them go find happiness.

Sometimes you might think that someone better is out there, so you keep the person you're only half interested in on the back burner while you see what happens with someone else. That's bad energy you're putting out into the world. If you can't look into a person's eyes and say that you love him or her, that's bad and will generate bad karma. You'll pay the price for that one later. You've just got to let the person go completely.

Move Out

Find a new place to live, if you have to. If you're living with your partner and you've given the relationship 100 percent but it's not working, it's time to move. How do you feel when you get home? Do you feel disconnected from yourself? Do you feel scattered, as though you're living in a tunnel and the light at the end of it is a train headed right toward you? Do you feel not free?

You can't stay in a relationship that isn't going to make you healthy and happy. When you're just not feeling happy or connected, no matter what you've tried to do to make the relationship work, it's time to move out and move on.

Saying Hello to Yourself Again

Get your ducks in a row. Ask yourself the following:

- What's best for me?
- What's healthy for me?
- Did trying to make this work make me a better person?
- Did trying to make this work just make me feel less guilty?

You probably already know the answers. But you have to do things to remind yourself that you've made the right choice. If you really weren't feeling good with that person, no matter how much you tried, the relationship had to end. If the connection isn't there anymore, then it won't come back, because it probably wasn't really there in the beginning. Maybe you were just trying extra hard to make it work because you hadn't been with someone in a really long time and this person was really nice and attentive.

> **People come into your life for a reason, and sometimes that reason is to help you open up for the right person. Never settle for second best.**

You don't become a better, stronger person by settling for less. People come into your life for a reason, and sometimes that reason is to help you open up for the right person. Never settle for second best. You want to have your cake and eat it, too. And no matter how guilty you might feel, letting guilt keep you in a relationship isn't fair to you or to the other person.

Remember what you learned about moving on after three dates: It's better to let people go quickly than to pretend that you want to be with them so they won't feel bad. It's better to let them move on with their lives, too, because if you're not feeling a good connection, they probably aren't, either.

Detox

If you've been in a relationship for a year or longer, you need to give yourself a minimum of three months to meditate and reconnect with yourself. Write down your thoughts and emotions. Get the bad ones out of you and focus on the thoughts and emotions that make you feel strong on your own.

You have your own power. Write that down: "I have my own power." If you need to, put it up where you will see it. It's true: you do have your own power. You came into this world alone, and you'll leave alone. You have strength enough to go it alone if you need to. So you've really got to get into your own power.

Take an entire weekend alone without technology: no texting, no e-mails, no talking on the phone, no surfing websites. You know how some people don't work on the weekends? That's what I want you to do: don't work; don't interact with anyone but yourself. Take a breather from being inundated with everyone else's business and focus on allowing yourself to be more connected, on a much deeper level, to yourself.

Take some time to read, meditate, and clean up your energy. Listening to music is okay, as long as it's music without words. I suggest either classical music or the sounds of nature—something that makes you feel both calm and hopeful. Particularly at the end of a long-term relationship, you may think there's no light at the end of the tunnel. If you think that, then there never will be. You have to take charge to change your own thought process.

If you project good energy, then good will come. If you project bad energy, then bad will come. Spend the weekend focused on thinking good thoughts and expelling bad thoughts. If you take the old and worn-out energy from the previous

> **If you project good energy, then good will come. If you project bad energy, then bad will come.**

relationship and bring it into the next one, you're not being fair to the new person. You have to really take the time to clear out the energy from the past relationship and focus on yourself.

Move Peacefully

Do something that involves moving your body—a yoga or Pilates class, a long hike, or a walk on the beach—and do it on a regular basis. Moving your body helps your energy flow more readily and clears out negative energy. Clearing your thoughts and your mind will make you feel more centered and connected to yourself.

It's important to reconnect with nature and do an exercise that helps you to be more mindful of your body—not of your weight or your strength, but of your actual muscles and bones. The aim is to reconnect with yourself spiritually. If you don't take care of your physical body, you won't be able to think about the spirit inside. Focus on being in nature because that is God's creation, just as you are. Connecting with a different element of God's creation will bring you closer to yourself.

Avoid Retail Therapy

I know many people who say that "retail therapy"—shopping—is their tried-and-true method for getting over things. It is definitely okay to go out and buy a new shirt and shoes when you're ready to date again, but right after a breakup you really need to be working on your inner spirit, not your outer wardrobe. It's much more important to create the space to be in line with yourself.

Don't try to bypass this stage. Pay attention to what you're really doing: avoiding the spiritual with the physical. You're actively choosing to focus only on the physical elements of yourself and on physical possessions rather than choosing to focus on the inside of the one you're with—yourself.

I know that it can be scary to be alone again, especially if you've been in a relationship for a while. But if you can't figure out how to love and respect the one you're with and get down to the nitty-gritty of being with yourself, how can you expect anyone else to?

Laugh It Up!

I know it sounds counterintuitive to tell you to laugh, especially if you're feeling sad, and it may be really hard to do if you're spending more time alone (intentionally or unintentionally). I suggest watching a funny movie that has minimal reference to love and love relationships. If you're really struggling to laugh, hop on the Internet and watch videos of babies laughing. It's almost impossible not to laugh when you see a baby laughing.

The reason it's important to laugh is that when you laugh on the outside, you're creating new space inside yourself. If you're not laughing on the outside, you won't be able to laugh on the inside; you won't be able to find joy in yourself or in other people. Finding joy in yourself is an important element of loving the one you're with, and it's also an incredibly important part of rediscovering any confidence you may have lost during the breakup.

Want to Be in a Relationship

Things will come in their own time. You'll heal and feel ready for a relationship again at your own pace. But part of *actually* being ready to reapproach dating is understanding whether you *want* to be in a relationship or just think that you *need* to be in a relationship. You don't need to be in one. Really. I don't care how many of your friends are married or what age you are or how fast your biological clock is ticking. You don't *need* to be in one. You don't *need* to meet anybody but yourself. All you need is to get connected to you.

Needing to be in a relationship means that you are desperate to be in one. You think that your life sucks and that it's going down the tubes unless you get into a relationship. You don't need to feel that way. When you have that kind of desperation, it means there's something inside you that you really need to work on. Take some time to figure out what that is.

I suggest that you take out a notebook and write down every relationship you've been in, starting with your very first kiss and working your way up to the most recent one. Write down how each relationship made you feel, what you saw, what you thought. Take time to look over what your patterns are and think about how to break them. And take some time to think about where those patterns came from—probably some past hurt that you haven't completely let go of and forgiven. It's time to let go now so that you can move on with your life.

When you are actually ready to be in a relationship, you will find that instead of thinking that you need to be in one because you feel uncomfortable about being alone or what other people think, you'll suddenly just want to be in one. Maybe you'll decide you're ready to open your heart up, or maybe you'll just meet someone great at the grocery store. Who knows what the future holds?

A Closing Thought

I'm excited for you and what you will learn and discover about yourself. I'm excited for you and the person you will find to spend the rest of your life with. It's an incredible thing to get to be with your soul mate, and it's an even more amazing thing to learn to love the one you're with. Keep up the good work of centering yourself and paying attention to the kinds of energetic connections that you feel. In everything you do, remember that we're not here for a long time, we're here for a good time!